T0332521

Computer Supported

Cooperative Work

An Introduction

Paul Wilson
CSC Europe

Advance Concepts Branch
CCTA

intellect
Oxford, England

First published in Great Britain in 1991 by
Intellect Books
Suite 2, 108/110 London Road, Oxford OX3 9AW

Published outside Great Britain by
Kluwer Academic Publishers
P.O. Box 17, 3300 AA Dordrecht, The Netherlands.

Sold and distributed in the U.S.A. and Canada by
Kluwer Academic Publishers
101 Philip Drive, Norwell, MA 02061, U.S.A.

Consulting editor: Masoud Yazdani
Copy editor: Cate Foster
Cover design: Steven Fleming

British Library Cataloguing in Publication Data

Wilson, Paul
  Computer supported cooperative work.
  I. Title
  650.028546

  ISBN 1-871516-26-9

Library of Congress Cataloging-in-Publication Data available

Printed and bound in Great Britain by Billing & Sons Ltd, Worcester

Contents

		Page
Chapter 1	**Management Summary**	**1**
Chapter 2	**Introduction**	**4**
	2.1 CSCW origins	4
	2.2 CCTA interest	4
	2.3 CSC Europe interest	5
	2.4 Objective of this publication	5
Chapter 3	**What is CSCW?**	**6**
	3.1 Definition of CSCW	6
	3.2 The emergence of CSCW	6
	3.3 The main components of CSCW	7
	3.4 Technology driving forces	8
	3.5 Business needs	9
	3.6 Products	9
	3.7 CSCW Associations and Special Interest Groups	11
	3.8 CSCW journals	12
	3.9 Electronic news sources	13
Chapter 4	**CSCW Research Activities**	**14**
	4.1 International programmes	14
	4.2 National programmes	17
	4.3 UK CSCW research	19
	4.4 Non-UK European CSCW research	20
	4.5 North American CSCW research	23
	4.6 CSCW research elsewhere in the world	25
Chapter 5	**Enabling Technologies**	**26**
	5.1 Categories of CSCW enabling technologies	26
	5.2 Infrastructure technologies	28
Chapter 6	**Group Process Aspects**	**30**
	6.1 Individual aspects	30
	6.2 Organisational aspects	31
	6.3 Group work design aspects	31
	6.4 Group dynamics aspects	32
Chapter 7	**The impact of CSCW on business and government**	**33**
	7.1 Timeline analysis	33
	7.2 Analysis of business and government needs	36
	7.3 Function analysis	39
Chapter 8	**CSCW benefits and risks**	**43**
	8.1 Benefits and risks of CSCW components	43
	8.2 CSCW benefits and risks with respect to business needs	44
	8.3 Benefits and risks of CSCW with respect to job functions	45
	8.4 Other benefits	46
	8.5 Other risks	47
Chapter 9	**Obtaining the benefits**	**48**
	9.1 Short-term initiatives	48
	9.2 Long-term goals	49
	9.3 Further advice on obtaining CSCW benefits	49

                                                                    Page

Appendix A   **Short descriptions of some products**   **50**

Appendix B   **Descriptions of research projects**   **56**
                 B.1 COST Co-Tech projects   56
                 B.2 ESPRIT projects   58
                 B.3 UK Advanced Technology Programme projects   60
                 B.4 Projects in the UK Joint Council initiative   61
                 B.5 National Science Foundation (NSF) projects   63
                 B.6 UK CSCW research   70
                 B.7 Non-UK European CSCW research   75
                 B.8 North American CSCW research   87
                 B.9 CSCW research elesewhere in the world   95

Appendix C   **Glossary**   **97**

Appendix D   **Useful Addresses and contacts**   **104**

Appendix E   **Recommended Reading**   **114**

Appendix F   **References**   **116**

                 Index   **120**

1 Management Summary

Computer Supported Cooperative Work (CSCW) is a generic term that combines the understanding of the way people work in groups with the enabling technologies of computer networking and associated hardware, software, services and techniques.

The support of group work has evolved naturally from a drive to increase personal productivity, and could lead to significant improvements in business efficiency and cost-effectiveness. The Advanced Concepts Branch of CCTA (the UK government centre for information systems) is evaluating CSCW technology and techniques to identify potential applications in government departments and to assess their potential benefits. This report has been produced to set the scene for the evaluation programme by providing a broad initial overview of the subject. As evaluation proceeds CCTA will publish more detailed assessments of specific aspects of CSCW.

As the aim of CSCW is to support group work effectiveness it has two major areas of concern: *the group working process*, and *the technology* that might be used to support it. The group work process, and other more more people-oriented aspects which are central to the problem of improving group efficiency, can be considered in 4 categories.
- *Individual human characteristics* such as conversation patterns and the making of commitments.
- *Organisational aspects* such as the structure and culture of organisations.
- *Group work design issues* such as user involvement in the work design process, rapid prototyping and usability testing.
- *Group dynamics aspects* such as group decision making and the collaboration process.

CSCW technology can also be considered in 4 categories.
- *Communication mechanisms* enabling people at different locations to see, hear and send messages to each other - for example, video conferencing and electronic mail.
- *Shared work space facilities* enabling people to view and work on the same electronic space at the same time - for example, remote screen sharing.
- *Shared information facilities* enabling people to view and work on a shared set of information - for example, multi-user databases.
- *Group activity support facilities* to augment group work processes - for example, the co-authoring of documents, and idea generation.

As an illustration of the relationship between enabling technologies and associated human issues, consider one of the simplest examples of support for groups - electronic mail. Here, the technologies of local and wide area networks linking desktop computers have created a new type of communication which supports new ways of group working and allows greater flexibility in the location and organisation of work.

Of course CSCW's scope is far greater than electronic mail: CSCW researchers and developers are harnessing a variety of technology developments including ISDN (Integrated Services Digital Network), and multi-media (incorporating voice, data, text, image and video). Potential applications for CSCW are also very wide in scope. For example:

- *collaboration tools* can help working groups agree what has to be done, allocate tasks and roles, and undertake specific group activities such as idea generation and group authoring. For example, the ability to obtain comments on draft documents in an organised way could be of immediate benefit in many organisations;
- *meeting room systems* can support face-to-face meeting activities such as the presentation and manipulation of information, decision making, minute taking and action review. Such systems could enable organisations to reduce the number of unproductive meetings; and to ensure that critical business processes such as strategic planning, produce the better results;
- *desktop video conferencing* enables two or more geographically separated people to interwork using a common screen display, video images of the other people in separate windows on the screen, and an integrated voice connection. Those who have to travel a great deal (senior management, for example) may find these systems to be of great use. Also, organisations which currently make use of video conferencing in dedicated rooms may find the desktop version a more convenient option;
- *procedure processing* or *work flow* technology can automate paper-based forms handling and, at the same time, provide full summary information about status, whereabouts and over-runs. Such systems will be of use to any organisation which finds itself hampered by the processing of large amounts of paper.

The cost of CSCW is very variable: some of the newer technologies such as desktop video conferencing or advanced meeting room systems, may require many thousands of pounds investment (though prices are likely to drop dramatically throughout the 1990s); whereas some network-based software products cost only a few hundred pounds. Consequently, care must be taken in the timing of the investment, and the perceived business benefits must be diligently pursued after implementation.

At the strategic level, CSCW benefits include the following.
- Opportunities for staff to work to their full potential.
- Fewer bottlenecks in communication, faster work turnaround.
- Faster decision making within and across organisational units.
- More thorough option analysis, improved quality of decisions.
- Reduced time to effect organisational changes.
- Faster product development and faster establishment of marketing and distribution infrastructures.
- Increased ability to support autonomous, interworking, groups.
- Improved quality of customer service.

In order to realise value from CSCW investments, organisations will need to identify specific aspects of their business which could benefit from improved group communications and teamwork. Government departments and other organisations which wish to investigate CSCW's potential might begin by undertaking pilot work on a real operational problem or challenge. Issues which might be addressed in such a pilot might include:

- the involvement of staff affected by the pilot, in its planning and design;
- the devolution of responsibility;
- the development of integrated solutions which encourage collaboration and cooperation;
- the use of physical mock-ups, software prototypes and practical usability testing;
- CSCW systems and products.

The Advanced Concepts Branch (ACB) is interested in exchanging experiences with organisations conducting such pilots, and would like to cooperate with other government departments and private sector bodies in the construction of a pilot scheme to evaluate the use of CSCW technology in government. This is likely to be in the areas of desktop conferencing and shared databases. The aim of the study will be to set up a working system for use within the department(s), and to assess it by various criteria to determine its value to government work and information systems.

In addition the ACB is evaluating specific CSCW tools and techniques, and is creating CSCW concept demonstrators. The evaluation results will be made available to central government departments and other interested organisations. Those wishing to view the concept demonstrators or to be kept informed of the ACB's evaluation work should contact the Advanced Concepts Branch (see Appendix D for a contact address).

2 Introduction

2.1 CSCW Origins

The 1980s saw a massive rise in the number of personal computers on people's desks. Following close behind was the trend to network these machines. As a result, there is a growing awareness of the possibilities for individuals to work together via networks, and of the need for specialised software to support specific group activities.

Independent of these developments, academics in niche areas such as decision support systems, coordination systems and office automation procedures, have been investigating the possibilities for providing computer support for groups in both face to face meetings and via networked systems. Other academics involved in sociology, anthropology, psychology and linguistics (to name just a few disciplines) have also been investigating how their subjects relate to work in a computerised world.

Finally, over the same time period, developments in Open Systems, Integrated Services Digital Networks (ISDN), display technology and workstation power have opened up a new world of possibilities for application developers.

Suddenly, in 1986 an international conference brought these various facets together. The aim was to discuss human group working preferences and characteristics, and to explore how they could be supported by computers. Participants immediately realised that the potent mix of disciplines and ideas had enormous potential, and since then the field of Computer Supported Cooperative Work (CSCW) has expanded rapidly.

Computer supplier organisations are interested because they foresee a new market in specialised software (already dubbed 'groupware'); network providers are interested because CSCW demands connectivity and high bandwidth; academics are interested because they foresee an opportunity to build usable systems based on an in-depth understanding of human individuals and groups; and user organisations are interested because in a changing world so much depends on the effective interworking of employee teams. These combined forces are now focused on the provision of computer support for groups. The results, already starting to emerge, will flood out in the latter half of the 1990s.

2.2 CCTA Interest

The mission of the UK government's computing agency, CCTA, is to supply knowledge and advice about the planning, implementation and use of Information Systems to help UK central government departments run their businesses effectively.

Much of CCTA's work concerns current and available technology. New technologies, however, have the potential to provide better solutions to business problems; so, if a prospective technique is likely to benefit government, then it is desirable to identify how those benefits can be achieved and to realise them as early as possible. Therefore, CCTA's Advanced Concepts Branch (ACB) undertakes wide ranging investigative and comparative work to assess upcoming technologies; and disseminates the knowledge and experience gained, throughout government departments. Commerce and industry also benefit from CCTA's advanced technology work since many of the outputs are made publicly available.

ACB's preliminary investigations have confirmed that Computer Supported Cooperative Work is an area which has considerable potential for improving the communications and effectiveness of work groups in government. A programme of detailed investigation and piloting work has now commenced, with the objective of identifying how CSCW can be used to best advantage and what benefits can be expected from it.

2.3 CSC Europe Interest

CSC Europe is part of an international organisation dedicated to serving clients in all aspects of Information Technology and Systems Integration. In this era of fast moving technology, CSC Europe monitors IT developments to assess their ability to provide cost effective solutions to business problems.

Of particular concern to many CSC Europe clients in both the public and private sectors, is the effectiveness of their workforces and their staff's ability to avoid the overheads of bureaucracy and to gain the benefits of effective teamwork. When CSC Europe first encountered CSCW in 1986, it seemed clear that this new field held out the prospect of solutions to such business concerns. So, to know more, CSC Europe became active in the research community, publishing a newsletter and organising the First European CSCW conference.

Now, at the beginning of the 1990s, the enabling technologies are becoming cheaper and more widely available, CSCW has become established as a research field in its own right and R&D groups in IT supplier organisations are working towards CSCW products. CSC Europe believes that CSCW products and techniques will provide significant benefits to organisations in the 1990s and beyond. Therefore, CSC Europe intends to stay abreast of developments, to feedback user requirements to the CSCW research community, and to help clients harness CSCW to improve the effectiveness of their key teams and processes and to re-engineer their businesses.

2.4 Objective of this Publication

The objective of this publication is to bring together in one volume the concepts, components, people and organisations that comprise the new field of CSCW. As such, it acts as an introductory handbook, first informing the reader of what CSCW is all about, and subsequently providing a source of reference information.

It is not intended to be a definitive volume - the field is already too large and changing too rapidly, to achieve that without a massive effort. However, readers should find it sufficient to gain a broad understanding of the field and to know where to go to find more.

The publication is aimed primarily at those who have responsibility for assessing new information technologies which might benefit their organisations. In addition, the book may also help those working in CSCW to assess the scope of the field and to relate their own work to that of others. This applies equally to researchers, developers, suppliers and practitioners.

3   What is CSCW?

3.1 Definition of CSCW

In 1984, Irene Greif (then at the Massachusetts Institute of Technology) and Paul Cashman (of Digital Equipment Corporation) decided to use the term "Computer Supported Cooperative Work" (CSCW) for a workshop they were running. In coining the term Greif and Cashman did not intend any special emphasis to the meaning of the individual words within it. They simply wanted a shorthand way of referring to a set of concerns about supporting multiple individuals working together with computer systems [1]. These concerns embraced everything from the different types of media that could be employed (text, voice, image, video), to the understanding of group processes.

This wide remit, coupled with the fact that it is still a very young field, makes it difficult to give a precise definition. However, for the purposes of this volume, CSCW is understood to be *a generic term which combines the understanding of the way people work in groups with the enabling technologies of computer networking and associated hardware, software, services and techniques* .This embraces a variety of other terms which have since appeared including 'Groupware' and 'Workgroup Computing'.

Groupware

Groupware is described by Robert Johansen in his book of the same name [2] as:

"...a generic term for specialised computer aids that are designed for the use of collaborative work groups. Typically, these groups are small project-oriented teams that have important tasks and tight deadlines. Groupware can involve software, hardware, services, and/or group process support."

Workgroup Computing

Workgroup Computing, on the other hand, tends to be used to describe support provided by the networked microcomputer[3]. Articles on Workgroup Computing usually restrict themselves to discussions of software products such as group calendars and shared telephone directories and files.

Although these various terms can all be said to represent CSCW in one form or another it is important to have an understanding of where their concepts and philosophies diverge. In this respect a key distinction is that Groupware and Workgroup Computing tend to be rather technology oriented, whereas CSCW prefers to assess how humans function prior to designing computer support for the group working process.

3.2 The Emergence Of CSCW

The first CSCW workshop run by Greif and Cashman in 1984 was only a small affair, but it convinced them that the subject was worth pursuing. So they set about organising the first conference on Computer Supported Cooperative Work (CSCW'86) at Austin, Texas, on 3-5 December 1986. Herb Krasner, the Conference Chair, told the 300 delegates that:

"..........much effort has been expended in search of the proper role in society for computer technology. This conference represents a refocusing of that role with the emphasis upon the cooperative working group and the computer technology which best supports it under various conditions of time and space." [4]

Krasner chose to use the word "refocusing" because most CSCW technologies and ideas had been around in one guise or another for several years: what was new was the gathering together of Sociologists, Anthropologists, Psychologists, Computer Scientists, Office Automation Specialists, Human Factors Specialists and Organisation Designers. Equally new was the combination and juxtaposition of topics such as Messaging Systems, Procedure Processing, Collaboration Research, Linguistics, Coordination Theory, Commitment Making, Group Processes, Face to Face Meeting Support, Decision Support Systems, Video Conferencing and Organisational Theory. The result was startling: it immediately became clear that the range of computer support that might be provided to work groups of all sizes is very great; and that, since organisations, by their very nature, rely on people working and cooperating together, CSCW's potential benefit could be huge.

The conference also made something else clear: CSCW tools will only work if they reflect and augment the way people actually talk, work and live together. This is more than just making the tools easy to use - their functionality must be derived from an accurate understanding of human traits, practices, communication and motivation.

CSCW'86 was a resounding success: those who had attended emerged with a new vision, and those who subsequently obtained the proceedings were inspired by the diversity of subject matter. Since then there has been a rapid growth of interest in CSCW around the world. The multidisciplinary nature of the subject has meant that large numbers of researchers and practitioners have found it to be of relevance and interest. New, more catchy names such as 'Workgroup Computing', 'Groupware', 'Technology for Teams' and 'Computer-Aided Teams' have emerged, and a whole variety of articles have appeared in all segments of the computer press.

CSCW Conferences

The second conference - CSCW'88 - was held in Portland, Oregon, in September 1988 and attracted 480 delegates; and the third - CSCW'90 - with 550 delegates was in Los Angeles in October 1990. The first European conference (EC-CSCW'89) took place at the Gatwick Hilton in September 1989 with 150 delegates. In the same year agreement was reached for the European and American events to be organised in alternate years with ECSCW'91 (a more manageable accronym) being held in Amsterdam, and CSCW'92 in Toronto, Canada. This level of activity indicates that CSCW has begun to emerge as a major research and development topic.

3.3 The Main Components Of CSCW

As CSCW aims to augment group effectiveness by using enabling technology, there are clearly two major areas of concern; firstly the group working process, and secondly the technology that might be employed to augment it. The components of each are described below.

Group Processes

In identifying the components of the group process area, it must first be remembered that groups operate via the contributions of individuals. Therefore, to understand and support group processes it is also necessary to understand and support the individual. Secondly, individuals and groups often work within organisational settings which place demands and constraints on what they do. Hence, CSCW must consider the organisational context in which group work is done. Thirdly, since the process of group work usually involves ongoing discussion between the participants about what to do, how to do it, and how to overcome problems, CSCW must also consider how the group work design process can be augmented. Finally, we must understand how people work together in groups (group dynamics), to be able to design appropriate support tools.

To summarise, therefore, the Group Processes area of CSCW can be considered under the following headings:
• individual aspects;
• organisational aspects;
• group work design aspects;
• group dynamics aspects.
Each of these is described in more detail in Chapter Six.

Enabling Technologies

The fundamental requirement for group work is communication - indeed most aspects of CSCW enabling technology could be said to be communication facilities of one sort or another. However, only those systems which simply provide a two-way channel between people (electronic mail and video conferencing for example) are referred to as 'communication systems' in this volume. Other systems which support the sharing of resources or add some organisation and structure to group communication are considered under separate headings.

Technologies that enable people to share resources can be considered in two categories: facilities that enable people to share information (multi-user databases for example), and facilities that enable people to share a physical work space (a remote screen sharing system, for example, which enables two or more people to work in a common area on their respective computer screens).

Finally, facilities that support specific group activities provide functionality for tasks such as idea generation, priority setting, and procedure processing. In summary, CSCW enabling technology can be considered under the following headings:
• communication systems;
• shared work space systems;
• shared information systems;
• group activity support systems.
Each of these is described in more detail in Chapter Five.

3.4 Technology Driving Forces

Continuing rapid developments in technology are providing opportunities for researchers to explore what is feasible, and for suppliers to create new markets. For example, there is no doubt that software supplier companies perceive multi-user, group-sharing applications across local area networks to be a potentially lucrative new market: and for researchers, improvements in video compression techniques and the power of processing chips now provide opportunities to explore workstation to workstation video conferencing.

There is little prospect of technology developments slowing down - indeed, if anything, they are now reaching a threshold at which relatively small improvements could create very great potential for improved and new group working tools. We can therefore expect that technology developments will continue to drive CSCW forward for some time to come.

3.5 Business Needs

The business trends of the 1980s - reduced overheads, flatter hierarchies, faster response, attention to customer needs - will continue to make dramatic demands on organisations in the 1990s. There is little doubt that the ability to secure new markets, and to retain market share, will become highly dependent on Information Technology (IT). In the face of such trends organisations are increasingly looking to:

• improve communication between people;
• reduce the time to make decisions;
• improve the quality of strategic decisions;
• make rapid changes in organisation structure;
• make faster moves into new markets;
• change and create products faster;
• reduce teamwork overheads and improve teamwork performance;
• improve the quality of service to customers.

Although CSCW has the potential to address these needs, too few products yet exist to demonstrate that CSCW can provide workable, affordable and easy to use solutions. In the meantime, organisations will become increasingly aware of the need for new tools to support their positions in rapidly changing marketplaces, and will express their needs for such products to suppliers.

3.6 Products

At the time of writing (in 1991), a comprehensive range of products based on CSCW principles did not exist. However, support for the collaborative work process could be obtained from products in a variety of different categories such as message systems, computer conferencing systems, procedure processing systems, calendar systems, shared filing systems, co-authoring systems, screen sharing systems, integrated group support packages, group decision support systems, advanced meeting room systems and team development and management tools. The costs of such products ranged from a few hundred pounds to many thousands of pounds. However, at the high end prices are likely to fall throughout the 1990s.

Descriptions of each product category are given below. Readers who wish to gain a clearer impression of what is available can read short descriptions of a few randomly selected products in Appendix A. To obtain up to date product listings readers should contact the CCTA Advanced Concepts Branch or CSC Europe.

Electronic Mail Systems

Electronic mail systems enable messages to be sent to one or more people. The messages are delivered to an electronic mailbox and are read at the time and location of the recipient's choosing. Electronic mail products (often referred to as 'email systems') have been available since the 1970s, although interconnection between proprietary products has been difficult. Now, though, the X.400 standard provides a framework for the interconnection of electronic mail systems and a global messaging environment. Most products are now being re-engineered to conform to this standard.

Computer Conferencing Systems

Computer conferencing systems are more structured versions of simple electronic mail: instead of messages being sent to one or more individuals, they are sent to 'activities' or 'conferences' or 'bulletin boards'. Users become members of specific conferences and upon selecting a particular conference are presented with all new material that they have not yet seen. Individuals can simply read the contents of conferences or reply to particular messages if they wish. All messages and replies are held in order within the conference and in this way 'conversations' are built up and can be reviewed as necessary. New users entering an already established conference are therefore able to 'catch up on the conversation' if they wish.

Procedure Processing/Work Flow Systems

Most large organisations maintain rule books defining procedures for everything from filling out an application for employment to completing an expense claim form. Some procedures are relatively small while others may have hundreds, even thousands, of logical statements. Most of them are eminently suited to computerisation. A procedure processing (or work flow) system will control the routing, advise of appropriate action to take upon receipt of an electronic form and provide status reports on all work in process[5].

Calendar Systems

Calendar systems provide individuals in a group with their own diary of events and activities, and with the ability to view the public parts of other people's diaries. Facilities are often provided to establish suitable meeting dates and to book agreed dates in the diaries of all concerned.

Shared Filing Systems

Shared filing systems enable individuals to create and access information in a shared database. Information can usually be designated as either public or private; and security features define who has the right to change specific parts of the file. Some systems enable links to be made between information held in the file (often referred to as hypertext systems) and in these cases individuals may be able to impose their own links on the information in addition to the public links provided for all users.

Co-authoring Systems

Co-authoring systems could, in principle, support all aspects of the joint creation of documents, from idea generation and outlining to peer review and version control. In fact relatively few products are currently available and none yet support the full range of activities just described.

Screen Sharing Systems

Screen sharing systems enable people using their own workstation to see what is on other people's screens - be they in the same building connected via a local area network, or in a remote location connected via a phone line or some other wide area network. Some products provide the ability to view and control another screen and to transfer files; while more sophisticated systems provide additional support for more structured types of work activity.

Integrated Group Support Packages

These packages typically run on local area networks and provide a range of common and integrated facilities to all the network users. Facilities often include electronic mail, word processing, spreadsheet, shared database, diary and meeting arrangement.

Group Decision Support Systems

Group Decision Support Systems (GDSS) have been defined as interactive computer-based systems which facilitate the solution of unstructured problems by a set of decision makers working together as a group[6]. Some GDSS are designed to be used in face-to-face meetings (often with each participant having the use of a computer), while others are for use when participants are in different locations[7]. GDSS often incorporate screen sharing features, but, in addition, possess functionality to support specific group activities such as prioritisation or voting. GDSS designed to support face-to-face meetings often require each participant to have the use of a computer and to be able to see a large public screen connected to the system. These kinds of systems are described below under the heading of 'Advanced Meeting Room Systems'.

Advanced Meeting Room Systems

Today's meeting room with table, chairs, whiteboard, overhead projector and 35 mm slides can be enhanced, if not transformed, by currently available products. Of particular significance is the ability to project a computer screen onto a meeting room wall screen so that information, graphics or presentation material can be displayed to meeting participants. Remote computers can be accessed via local or wide area networks, as can remote Value Added Services such as on-line databases. Work done during meetings can be displayed as it is input - meeting minutes for example, or spreadsheet what-if scenarios. More sophisticated arrangements provide a computer for each meeting participant and a range of meeting support software.

Team Development and Management Tools

While the majority of CSCW products support the collaborative process itself, a few aim to support the establishment and management of groups. Examples of facilities provided include the analysis of group interactivity based on individual responses to questionnaires; and project planning and management.

3.7 CSCW Associations and Special Interest Groups

Although very few organisations dedicated to CSCW currently exist, many groups embrace the field. In particular the Office Information Systems Special Interest Group of the Association of Computing Machinery (ACM) has been associated with the subject since the first CSCW conference in 1986. The address for this group is included in Appendix D (look under ACM).

Two organisations dedicated solely to CSCW were identified in the course of writing this volume: the Foundation for Cooperative Work Technology, and a UK CSCW Special Interest Group.

Foundation for Cooperative Work Technology (FCWT)

The FCWT is a loose confederation of organisations that have a special interest in CSCW. Its primary initial aims are to provide long-term continuity for the European CSCW conference, to facilitate the distribution of prototype software among CSCW researchers, and to promote and try out the concept of a collaboratory - a virtual electronic work environment without walls but fully equipped with a range of CSCW tools to enable the distributed participants to interact together as effectively as if they were co-located.

A contact address for the FCWT is provided in Appendix D (look under Foundation).

UK CSCW SIG

The UK Human Interface (HI), and Communications & Distributed Systems (CDS) Clubs established a joint CSCW Special Interest Group in February 1990. The HI and CDS Clubs were created to support participants in the Alvey research programme, and continue to be supported by the Directors of the UK Government's Advanced Technology Programme (see Chapter 4 Section 2 for a description of this Programme). The objectives of the Clubs are to:
- promote and maintain cohesion of the UK effort in their respective fields;
- facilitate technology transfer from the research community to the commercial user community;
- establish a strong UK base from which to participate fully and effectively in European research programmes.

The aim of the CSCW SIG is to provide a focus for the UK CSCW community by organising seminars and workshops, maintaining an up to date membership/mailing list, providing information about ongoing projects and events, publishing CSCW material and providing an electronic service for information, discussion and communication. A contact address for this group is included in Appendix D (look under CSCW Special Interest Group).

3.8 CSCW Journals

Two journals dedicated to CSCW and related issues emerged in the early 1990s - one called *Computer Supported Cooperative Work* and the other called *The Journal of Organizational Computing* (these are described in more detail below). In addition the journal *Group Decision and Negotiation* (ISSN 0926-2644) will address topics closely related to CSCW when it is launched in 1992 (the address of the publisher, Kluwer Academic, is provided in Appendix E).

Finally, journals such as the ACM *Transactions on Information Systems* (ISSN 1046-8188) (an address is provided in Appendix D under ACM) and the *International Journal of Man-Machine Studies* (ISSN 0020-7373) (an address is provided in Appendix D under Academic Press) maintain a close interest in CSCW and have published special CSCW issues (listed in Appendix E).

Computer Supported Cooperative Work Journal (ISSN 0925-9724)

This international journal, launched in 1992 by Kluwer Academic Publishers, is a quarterly interdisciplinary forum for the latest theoretical and empirical work in CSCW; for the discussion, critique and development of underlying concepts and methodology; and for exchanging ideas, difficulties and dilemmas in technological support for cooperative working. The journal is edited by an international collective, the founding members of which are Liam Bannon, John Bowers, Charles Grantham, Mike Robinson, Kjeld Schmidt and Susan Leigh Star. A contact address for this journal is included in Appendix D (see under Kluwer Academic).

Journal of Organizational Computing
ISSN 1054-1721

The Journal of Organizational Computing is a quarterly journal launched in 1991 by Ablex Publishing. It publishes original research articles concerned with the impact of computer and communication technology on organisational design, operations and performance. The journal's editorial areas are CSCW, groupware, computer modeling of organisations, investigations of organisational systems issues such as computer-aided coordination and organisational learning, organisational computing economics, and behavioral studies of organisational computing. The journal publishes theoretical, experimental and survey research, as well as book reviews and meeting announcements. The Founding Editor is Andrew Whinston with Associate Editors Lynda Applegate, Clyde Holsapple, Clarence Ellis and Franz Radermacher.

A contact address for this journal is included in Appendix D (see under Ablex).

3.9 Electronic News Sources

Within the electronic networks of the world a great deal of news and information is distributed via formal or semi-formal electronic newsletters, bulletin boards and mailings. At least two such facilities are available for CSCW; the Usenet 'Comp/Groupware' Newsgroup mailing, and the UK CSCW SIG's computer conferences within the HICOM service.

Usenet Comp/Groupware Newsgroup

Usenet is a network of over 10,000 machines which communicate by the unix UUCP system. The network transmits the News - an electronic bulletin board to which individuals can submit items to be read by tens of thousands of people worldwide. The News is split into news-groups, and users of a receiving machine can subscribe to any or all of them. One news-group is called Comp/Groupware; it carries a wide variety of information including general discussion, conference announcements, research initiatives, etc.

A contact address for USENET is included in Appendix D.

CSCW SIG HICOM Computer Conferences

Hicom is a UK communication and information service for all those from academia, professional bodies and industry alike, who are interested in Human-Computer Interaction (HCI). Hicom is owned and managed by the HCI community for the HCI community. The UK CSCW SIG uses Hicom to provide an electronic environment for members to share information and discuss CSCW issues.

Contact addresses for HICOM and CSCW SIG are provided in Appendix D.

4 CSCW Research Activities

CSCW research is underway in most western countries and in many supplier organisations. Although much of this activity is a continuation of work previously undertaken under different names, it is clear that the establishment of CSCW as a concept in its own right has given added focus and impetus to these efforts.

Although much is already happening - as is apparent from the reports elsewhere in this chapter - growth in new CSCW research projects is still strong, and this trend is expected to continue for some time. The growing tide of results from these efforts should have an increasing impact on supplier and user organisations over the remainder of the 1990s.

This chapter provides a snapshot of current CSCW research activity. It is not a definitive statement, nor is it comprehensive. But, nevertheless, it does indicate the scale and scope of what is going on. Activities in international and national programmes are listed first, followed by research being undertaken in specific organisations within the UK, non-UK European countries, the USA, and elsewhere in the world. Addresses for the contact names provided can be found in Appendix D. Fuller descriptions of the research projects are provided in Appendix B. Much of the project information was contributed by the researchers themselves, and thanks are due to them for their assistance.

4.1 International Programmes

Only three international programmes undertaking substantial CSCW work were known of at the time of writing. All are limited to cooperation between European countries. One is called CO-TECH and operates within the framework of COST. Two other European Programmes - ESPRIT and RACE - include some CSCW projects within their much broader remits. Descriptions of these programmes are provided below:

COST 14 CO-TECH Action

COST is a framework for cooperation in science and technology between European Community countries and other countries in Europe. Some COST actions provide limited funding for the travel and subsistence costs of meetings and exchanges of the participants, and typically run for three years or more. Participants are expected to make their own arrangements through their national bodies to cover the time and materials expenses of COST projects.

Development of proposals for a COST CSCW programme (to be known as Co-Tech) started in 1989 and led to the establishment of of a number of Working Groups, each addressing a potential COST CSCW project. This exercise in itself was sufficient to establish an identifiable community of European CSCW researchers. By the beginning of 1991 plans were in place for a full COST Co-Tech programme to be established by the beginning of 1992. Should these plans come to fruition the programme is likely to be based around the topics being addressed by the following working groups.

- Information Technology support for Group Knowledge development (ITSforGK).
- An environment for CSCW applications.
- Cooperative Multi-media processes: the impact of organisational, spatial and temporal factors (COMMPOSITE).
- Developing CSCW systems: design concepts (DECO).
- Interdisciplinary theoretical approaches for Cooperation Technology (INTACT).
- Reference model for CSCW systems support.
- Distributed meetings.
- User centred requirements for a multi-media interface in performing cooperative tasks (U-CERAMICS).

Descriptions of these projects, and a contact name for each, are included in Appendix B of this volume. If the Co-Tech Action does proceed a formal link may be established with ESPRIT basic research (see below).

Co-Tech Contact   Rolf Speth.

ESPRIT CSCW Research   ESPRIT (the European Strategic Programme for Research & Development in Information Technologies) started in 1984 and is part of the European Community's Framework Programme of collaborative research and development. The Framework Programme encompasses a variety of domains, including Information Technology, Industrial Technology, Marine Science, Agriculture, the Life Sciences etc. ESPRIT provides support for IT research projects undertaken collaboratively by organisations based in different European Community countries. Most years an annual work programme is produced which acts as a call for pre-competitive collaborative project proposals.

ESPRIT CSCW-Related Projects   The following recently completed or current ESPRIT projects are relevant to CSCW.
- MULTIWORKS: Development of a multimedia workstation.
- ISEM: IT support for emergency management.
- ELO: Elusive office.
- KWICK: Knowledge workers intelligently collecting, coordinating and consulting knowledge.
- MIAS: Multipoint interactive audio-visual system.
- EUROCOOP: IT support for distributed cooperative work.
- PECOS: Perspectives on cooperative systems.
- IMAGINE: Integrated multi-agent interactive environment.

Descriptions of these projects, and a contact name for each, are included in Appendix B of this volume.

ESPRIT 1991 Call for Proposals   The 1991 Work Programme invited proposals for one major CSCW project under the heading of *The Cooperative Working Shell*. The shell is an application-independent software layer which has the core functionality to tailor specific applications and to support cooperative working across a range of application domains. Approved projects resulting from the 1991 call were planned to start in 1992.

Esprit Contact   Attilio Stajano.

Esprit Basic CSCW Research

In addition to pre-competitive collaborative projects, ESPRIT also runs a programme of more fundamental 'basic' research. It is possible that some CSCW projects may be funded in the early 1990s within the basic research programme; and that some of those projects may have a direct link with any COST Co-Tech projects that are initiated (See COST Co-Tech Action above).

Esprit Basic Research Contact

George Metakides.

RACE

RACE (Research and Development in Advanced Communications technologies in Europe) is also part of the European Community's Framework Programme of collaborative research and development. RACE is focused on the development of advanced communications technology for the introduction of commercial Integrated Broadband Communications (IBC) services in Europe in 1995. The 1.1 billion ECU programme was started in January 1988. About 2000 leading experts are collaborating in joint teams on 85 projects, sharing work, experiences and results. Participants include telecommunications and information technology equipment manufacturers, user organisations, most major research establishments, many small enterprises and numerous universities.

Future telecommunications services depend on international and widespread user acceptance more than ever before. RACE involves special activities to stimulate a dialogue between organisations using telecommunications, service providers, network operators and technologists; and to contribute to the emergence of a broad consensus on requirements and objectives. These activities are complemented by a number of application pilots exploring ways to meet present and future demand, to limit investment risks and to accelerate the introduction of a broadband infrastructure in Europe. The first phase of the RACE programme includes 17 application pilots in manufacturing industry, healthcare, transport, banking, finance and insurance, and media, publishing and culture.

RACE Advanced Communication Experiments (ACE)

The Operation 1992 Advanced Communications R&D planning exercise identified the opportunity to supplement the initial set of RACE pilots with an extended and structured range of Advanced Communication Experiments (ACE's). The objectives of the experiments are to enable users to determine the benefits and opportunities provided by advanced communications technology in a realistic experimental environment, and to provide inputs on usage characteristics to compare with the assumptions made during the development of the basic technology and system engineering. The set of experiments are structured in such a way to increase the understanding of how advanced communications will benefit and change business. ACE projects address 11 different generic applications.
- Distributed case handling.
- Inter-personal communications.
- Remote delivery of expertise.
- Distributed collaborative decision making.
- Distributed learning / training.
- Monitoring and surveillance.

- Telemarketplace.
- Entertainment / leisure distribution.
- Multimedia inter-personal messaging.
- Multimedia information assembly / access.
- Distributed collaborative design.

A call for proposals for ACE projects was issued in mid-1991. The work is being carried out over the period 1991 - 1995, and consists of a series of user-focused trials, in live environments.

RACE Contact   Jose Torcato.

4.2 National Programmes

Three national programmes containing CSCW projects were known of at the time of writing. Two are in the UK and one is in the USA:

The UK Advanced Technology Programme

The UK Advanced Technology Programme (ATP) is jointly managed by the Information Engineering Directorate - a division of the UK Government's Department of Trade & Industry - and the UK Science & Education Research Council (SERC). It contains three main areas of work.
- systems engineering;
- systems architecture;
- silicon microelectronics.

The first ATP call for proposals was issued in June 1988, the second in June 1989, and the third in September 1990. CSCW-related projects funded as a result of these calls include.
- establishing the communicational requirements of IT systems that support humans cooperating remotely;
- aide-de-camp (facilitating the cooperative working of dispersed teams);
- cooperative requirements capture;
- multimedia user modelling systems.

Descriptions of these projects, and a contact name for each, are included in Appendix B of this volume.

UK ATP Contact   David Hutchison

The UK Joint Council initiative in Cognitive Science and Human-Computer Interaction

This initiative is being conducted jointly by three UK research funding councils: the Economic and Social Research Council (ESRC), the Medical Research Council (MRC), and the Science and Engineering Research Council (SERC). The programme started in 1990 and will last for 5 years. Calls for project proposals are issued at yearly intervals. The following eleven research themes have been chosen for the programme.
- Systems design
  - tools, methods and the design process;
  - linking language to image.
- Principles of interaction
  - models of users in interaction with the system;
  - modelling of communication and collaboration among active agents;
  - representation of organisational knowledge.

- Computational learning environments
  - effects on learning of the forms of presentation, action and feedback;
  - intelligent tutoring;
  - support of programming.
- Computational modelling of cognition
  - models of cognition and learning;
  - general theoretical principles of 'network' models;
  - psychophysics and modelling of neural phenomena, especially low-level vision and speech.

CSCW-related projects that have been funded by the Joint Council Initiative include:
- a distributed artificial intelligence based investigation into the emergence of social complexity;
- a multidisciplinary exploration of the problem of joint action;
- the development of a cognitive model for computer support of collaborative writing;
- social knowledge representation: an anthropological perspective;
- interactive generative organisational frame of reference.

Descriptions of these projects, and a contact name for each, are included in Appendix B of this volume.

UK Joint Council Initiative contact

Elizabeth Pollitzer.

The USA National Science Foundation Initiative in Coordination Theory and Collaboration Technology

This initiative is funded by the US National Science Foundation (NSF) Information Technology and Organizations Program. The Program is part of the Information, Robotics & Intelligent Systems Division of the Computer and Information Science and Engineering Research Directorate. The objective of the initiative is to stimulate multidisciplinary research that may lead to new knowledge about human and machine coordination and the technology to support collaboration. Three scientific issues of particular concern for coordination and collaboration are:
- to discover principles underlying how people collaborate and coordinate work efficiently and productively in environments characterized by a high degree of decentralized computation and decision-making;
- to increase fundamental knowledge about the structure and outputs of organisations, industries and markets which incorporate sophisticated, decentralized information and communications technology as a component of their operations;
- and to understand problems of coordination in decentralized or open computer and communication systems.

The initiative started in 1989 and, up to the time of writing, had awarded two sets of grants: in 1989 six projects (out of a total of 48 proposals received) were funded at a total cost of $4,100,000 over a three-year period; and in 1990 eleven additional projects (out of 86 submitted proposals) costing $4,591,900 over three years were funded. The projects are:
- academic institutional memory: analyzing the electronic artifacts of scientific culture;

- a normative-descriptive theory of coordination in distributed organizations;
- representing and supporting coordination.
- coordinating multi-processor organizations.
- the "work in preparation"(PREP) editor: support for co-authoring and commenting;
- technology support for collaborative workgroups;
- coordination of distributed decision making in a corporate planning environment;
- flexible coordination in collaborative software engineering;
- a hierarchical negotiation protocol using multi-dimensional behaviour specifications;
- supporting collaborative design with integrated knowledge-based design environments;
- decision-making based on practical knowledge;
- distributed group support systems;
- real time, interactive information systems;
- fractal interfaces for collaborative work;
- systems technology for building a national collaboratory;
- building and using a collaboratory: a foundation for supporting and studying group collaborations;
- distributed concurrent hypertext for multi-reader cooperative systems.

Descriptions of these projects, and a contact name for each, are included in Appendix B of this volume.

NSF contact   Laurence Rosenberg.

4.3 UK CSCW   Some of the organisations undertaking CSCW research in the UK
Research   are listed below. Fuller descriptions of the work they are doing are
                         provided in Appendix B.

BICC   Multimedia and desktop video conferencing for distributed
Technologies   manufacturing design.
                         Location: Hemel Hempstead. Contact: Chris Condon.

BNR Europe Ltd   The Professional Community Support (PCS) Programme includes
                         work on MULTIWORKS (Multimedia Integrated Workstations),
                         and software architectures for group process support.
                         Location: Harlow. Contact: Philip Hughes.

Brunel University   Research into the impact of social and organisational issues on
                         knowledge engineering and information systems design.
                         Location: Uxbridge. Contact: Duska Rosenberg.

CSC Europe   Investigations into support for distributed groups and organisation,
                         desktop video conferencing implementation issues, and group
                         knowledge development.
                         Location: Slough. Contact: Paul Wilson.

Hewlett-Packard   Research into the use and effectiveness of multimedia
Laboratories   communications and desktop video conferencing.
                         Location: Bristol. Contact: Stephen Gale.

Loughborough University of Technology	Project on 'Establishing the communication requirements of IT systems that support humans cooperating remotely' (concentrating on the graphic design application domain). Location: Loughborough. Contact: Steve Scrivener.
Queen Mary & Westfield College, University of London	QMW is building a multimedia environment for the development and evaluation of applications to support a range of remote cooperative activities. Location: East London. Contact: Sylvia Wilbur.
Rank Xerox EuroPARC	EuroPARC has built an integrated multimedia and computational environment to provide the infrastructure for research into interactivity and connectivity in different media. Location: Cambridge. Contact: Bob Anderson.
UMIST	The development of a methodology for user-centred requirements capture, and software tools to provide cooperative support for the requirements capture and analysis process. Location: Manchester. Contact: Linda Macaulay.
University of Lancaster	Multi-disciplinary CSCW research involving the computing and sociology departments. Projects have addressed network management as a cooperative activity, air traffic control, police work, database requirements for CSCW, and cooperative design. Location: Lancaster. Contact: Tom Rodden.
University of Manchester	The Psychology Department is developing a design methodology for CSCW systems and is researching social psychological aspects of computer mediated communication and networking. Location: Manchester. Contact: John Bowers.
University of Nottingham	The Communications Research Group, in the Department of Computer Science, is exploring the use of OSI protocols to provide infrastructures for CSCW systems. The Psychology Department is researching multimedia tools to support synchronous distributed problem solving; and the software development process in large design teams. Location: Nottingham. Contacts: Hugh Smith and Claire O'Malley.
University of Sussex	Research into computer supported collaborative writing. Location: Brighton. Contact: Mike Sharples.

4.4 Non-UK European CSCW Research

Some of the organisations undertaking CSCW research in Europe, excluding the UK, are listed below. Fuller descriptions of the work they are doing are provided in Appendix B.

Delft University of Technology	The Psychology department is investigating user requirements for multi-media applications, computer supported communication in work organisations, and CSCW tools which support asynchronous and synchronous communication. Location: Delft, The Netherlands. Contact: J.H. Erik Andriessen.

ETH - the Swiss Federal Institute of Technology

ETH is working on the MultimETH conferencing system that supports real-time multimedia (image, text and voice, but not video) communication between distributed workstations using internationally standardised protocols.
Location: Zürich, Switzerland. Contact: Hannes P. Lubich.

GMD (Gesellschaft fur Mathematik und Datenverarbeitug)

GMD's "Assisting Computer (AC)" project is developing a new generation of support systems, an essential characteristic of which will be its support for cooperation. The research focuses on the support of asynchronous collaboration in situations ranging from official procedures to more informal ways of working.
Location: Bonn, Germany. Contact: Peter Hoschka.

Joint Research Centre of CEC, Ispra

CSCW research work at Ispra is focused on 'enabling technologies' for supporting the use of multimedia real-time desktop conferencing by geographically dispersed users.
Location: Ispra, Italy. Contact: Adriano Endrizzi.

Risoe National Laboratory

The Cognitive Systems Group is actively involved in the development of experimental CSCW systems in conjunction with theoretical studies and field studies of cooperative work in complex work domains.
Location: Roskilde, Denmark. Contact: Kjeld Schmidt.

RSO

RSO is developing a methodology to design cooperative networks. It also founded its 'Laboratory for Cooperation Technologies' in 1988 with the aim of observing, evaluating and testing cooperation technologies. Location: Milan, Italy. Contact: Thomas Schael.

Swedish Institute of Computer Science (SICS)

SICS is working on models for cooperative work, the support of distributed multimedia computer systems and the development of a distributed mobile workstation with supporting applications.
Location: Stockholm, Sweden. Contact: Bjorn Pehrson.

TA-Triumph-Adler

Triumph-Adler's research department is investigating the provision of support for distributed collaborative work, with a special focus on the use of portable computers.
Location: Nuernberg, Germany. Contact: Klaus Kreplin.

Technical Research Centre of Finland

The Laboratory for information Processing is working on the DISSPRO project which is investigating management, communication and collaboration issues within the software development process.
Location: Helsinki, Finland. Contact: Sakari Kalliomaki.

Technical University of Aachen

The Department of Computer Science is investigating knowledge-based support for distributed cooperation in co-authoring and software development.
Location: Aachen, Germany. Contact: Stefan Eherer.

Technical University of Madrid

The department of Telematic Systems Engineering is taking part in the PECOS project which is investigating the modelling of cooperative situations and the process of designing CSCW support tools. It is also working on OSI-based architectures for distributed cooperative activities.
Location: Madrid, Spain. Contact: Encarna Pastor.

Technical University of Vienna

The department of Applied Computer Science is developing principles for CSCW product development.
Location: Vienna, Austria. Contact: Brigitte Haberkorn.

University of Aarhus

The Computer Science Department is working on tools and techniques for the support of system development as a cooperative activity, with special emphasis on end-user/developer cooperation, and on object-orientation.
Location: Aarhus, Denmark. Contact: Morten Kyng.

University of Amsterdam

The Centre for Innovation & Co-operative Technology is working on the Amsterdam Meeting Environment (AME). AME is designed to support face-to-face meetings dealing with issues for which there are no 'correct' solutions.
Location: Amsterdam, The Netherlands. Contact: Mike Robinson.

University College Dublin

The department of Computer Science is developing collaborative business applications, and is investigating the design, development and management of infrastructure platforms on which to support such applications. Location: Dublin, Republic of Ireland.
Contact: Michael Sherwood-Smith.

University of Geneva

Geneva's Centre Universitaire d'Informatique is interested in the cooperative nature of object-oriented software development.
Location: Geneva, Switzerland. Contact: Simon Gibbs.

University of Hohenheim

Hohenheim is developing the Computer Aided Team Room (CATeam Room) to support group work consisting of a mix of phased tasks which may be accomplished by face-to-face meetings or by group members working separately.
Location: Hohenheim, Germany. Contact: Helmut Krcmar.

University of Jyvaskyla

The Department of Computer Science and Information Systems is developing its SAMPO approach for the analysis of cooperative work processes and for the design of appropriate computer support systems. Automated tools to support the SAMPO method are also being developed.
Location: Jyvaskyla, Finland. Contact: Kalle Lyytinen.

University of Karlsruhe

Karlsruhe's Institute for Telematics is working with the University of Kaiserslautern's Telematics Working Group to provide development and runtime support for cooperative applications in a distributed environment.
Location: Karlsruhe, Germany. Contact: Tom Ruedebusch.

University of Lund

CSCW work at the Department of Information & Computer Science aims to identify the types of computer support that will promote cooperation in the work place; and to assess how such computer support should be designed and applied.
Location: Lund, Sweden. Contact: Agneta Olerup.

University of Milan	The Department of Computer Science is working on the concept that language and speech can be equated to physical action, and that the commitments and responsibilities uttered in speech can be recorded in a knowledge base and used to structure subsequent mail-based communication within a group. Location: Milan, Italy. Contact: Giorgio De Michelis.
University of Roskilde	Roskilde's Department of Computer Science is working on consensus journals - a method of scientific communication that has the economy of invitational journals and the objectivity of journals based upon peer review. That is, all articles are published and the reader benefits from article selection based upon impartial refereeing. Location: Roskilde, Denmark. Contact: David S. Stodolsky.
University of Stockholm	Stockholm's Department of Psychology is undertaking the CAFKA project which focuses on the way knowledge-based systems act as a communication mechanism between domain specialists and end users; and the AIDAI project which is analysing communication difficulties between system designers and end users. Location: Stockholm, Sweden. Contact: Yvonne Waern.
University of Trento	Trento's Computer Science Institute is working on group decision making, hypertext systems, organisational behaviour and the cooperative aspects of game theory. Location: Trento, Italy. Contact: Luisa Mich.
University of Twente	Twente's School of Management Studies has a research team working on the 'upstream' end of the software engineering process. The research is largely based on the modelling of organisations as systems of social norms. Location: Twente, The Netherlands. Contact: Ronald Stamper.

4.5 North American CSCW Research

Some of the organisations undertaking CSCW research in North America are listed below. Fuller descriptions of the work they are doing are provided in Appendix B.

Bellcore	To investigate the role of informal and formal communications in the workplace, Bellcore undertakes a variety of projects ranging from co-authoring to the use of desktop and large screen video systems. Location: New Jersey & elsewhere, USA. Contact: Robert Kraut.
Digital Equipment Corporation (DEC)	Since the mid 1980s DEC has been developing coordination systems to support the software development process. More recently it has been researching the provision of support for group meetings. Location: Stow, Massachesetts, USA. Contact: David Marca.
Florida International University	The School of Computer Science is investigating the role of communication among collaborative agents. Location: Miami, Florida, USA. Contact: Christian Stary.
Hewlett-Packard Laboratories	In addition to researching collaborative multimedia systems, HP Labs is also investigating technologies that enable teams to improve their management of computer-based conversations. Location: Palo Alto, California, USA. Contact: Allan Kuchinsky.

Institute for the Future (IFTF)	IFTF's Outlook Project is investigating market trends relating to CSCW, including competitive information, sales trends and forecasts. IFTF is also conducting research into the early field experiences of companies trying out CSCW systems and concepts. Location: Menlo Park, California, USA. Contact: Robert Johansen.
Massachusetts Institute of Technology	The MIT Center for Coordination Science conducts multidisciplinary research to develop new theories of coordination; to develop new collaborative tools; and to understand how current group work practices might be affected by new collaborative tools. Location: Boston, Massachusetts, USA. Contact: Thomas Malone.
MCC	Since the mid-1980s MCC's Software Technology Program has been investigating a variety of CSCW technologies including electronic meeting rooms, real-time multiuser group outline editors, and issue-based information systems. Current CSCW research efforts are focused on systems to support coordination among people tasks, and resources in an organisation. Location: Austin, Texas, USA. Contact: Gail Rein.
Queen's University	The School of Business has been studying the use of group decision support tools in face-to-face electronic meeting rooms, since the mid-1980s. Location: Kingston, Ontario, Canada. Contact: Brent Gallupe.
University of British Columbia	The MIS Division of the Faculty of Commerce is examining the behavioural effects (at the individual, group and organisational levels) of supporting face-to-face and distributed groups with computer technology. The design of the human-computer interface for CSCW applications is also being researched. Location: Vancouver, Canada. Contact: V. Srinivasan (Chino) Rao.
University of Calgary	The Department of Computer Science is investigating various types of real-time support for distributed groups, including the sharing of applications and the use of group sketching tools. Other work is being done on asynchronous group writing and the integration of conventional electronic mail with repertory grid elicitation. Location: Calgary, Alberta, Canada. Contact: Saul Greenberg.
University of Georgia	The Department of Management is investigating six aspects of computer-augmented teamwork: comparison of team technologies, facilitation and leadership, team development, team creativity, cross-cultural analysis, and adoption and diffusion of team technology. Location: Athens, Georgia, USA. Contact: Rick Watson.
University of Houston	The Information Systems Research Center in the College of Business Administration is carrying out a critical review of CSCW literature and research; a survey of the use of groupware in industry and government in Houston; and research into group decision support systems. Location: Texas, USA. Contact: Rudy Hirschheim.

University of Michigan

The Cognitive Science & Machine Intelligence Lab (CSMIL) conducts research on a variety of topics in CSCW. Much of the current work focuses on synchronous collaboration, both face-to-face and distributed, and is a mixture of field studies and laboratory research The Collaboration Technology Suite (CTS) is a special research facility for this work.
Location: Ann Arbor, Michigan, USA. Contact: Gary Olson.

University of Oakland

Oakland's School of Business Administration is studying the use of CSCW in small business environments; the use of CSCW to help overcome management problems in integrated manufacturing systems; and systems for the ordering of group opinions.
Location: Rochester, Michigan, USA. Contact: Robbin R. Hough.

University of Texas

The Laboratory for Organisational Computing is researching the organisation of the future by experimenting with organisational forms, tasks and processes, and by building groupware support for specific application requirements.
Location: Austin, Texas, USA. Contact: Andrew Whinston.

University of Toronto

Toronto's Computer Science Department is developing multi-modal communication support between personal workstations to enhance collaboration on complex work projects that take place at a distance.
Location: Toronto, Canada. Contact: Marilyn Mantei.

Xerox Palo Alto Research Centre (PARC)

PARC has a substantial programme of CSCW research investigating varied aspects of work practices (from an anthropological perspective) and a wide variety of technologies to support group activities.
Location: Palo Alto, California, USA. Contact: Lucy Suchman.

4.6 CSCW Research Elsewhere in the World

Some of the organisations undertaking CSCW research outside Europe and North America are listed below. Fuller descriptions of the work they are doing are provided in Appendix B.

National Chiao Tung University

The Institute of Information Management is researching four basic areas: coordination theory, human-computer networks, organisational structures and coordination technology.
Location: Hsinchu, Taiwan. Contact: Keh-Chiang Yu.

National University of Singapore

The Department of Information Systems and Computer Science (DISCS) is studying the influence of cross-cultural differences among nationals on Group Decision Support Systems (GDSS) theory and design, and is developing a GDSS suited for use in collectivistic Asia-Pacific cultures.
Location: Singapore. Contact: K.S.Raman.

NTT

NTT is working on new telecommunication services based on the Integrated Services Digital Network (ISDN). Systems being researched involve desktop video conferencing and shared workspaces. Heavy emphasis is placed on human interface issues.
Location: Kanagawa, Japan. Contact: Hiroshi Ishii.

5 Enabling Technologies

5.1 Categories of CSCW Enabling Technologies

Four categories of CSCW enabling technologies were identified in Chapter Three:
• communication systems;
• shared work space systems;
• shared information systems;
• group activity support systems.

These are not mutually exclusive - a CSCW system might possess facilities in any combination of the categories. For example, a distributed meeting system might display video images of participants in windows on each person's screen (a communication system), provide a common shared screen area which all participants can see and use (a shared work space), make use of brainstorming software to generate ideas and options (a group activity support facility), and provide a shared database of information relevant to the meeting (a shared information facility).

Communication Systems

People talk and interact together in informal and unstructured ways. For example, when they gather together in a room to chat and mingle, people can see, hear, smell and bump against other people merely by being present. When a face-to-face gathering is not feasible however, technological support can be provided to enable informal communication to continue - albeit at a reduced level of effectiveness, naturalness and flexibility (though one of CSCW's main aims is to build communication systems which match the enhanced characteristics of the face-to-face environment).

Examples of communication systems being developed in CSCW research are:
• advanced electronic mail systems (incorporating advanced computer conferencing facilities, and support for graphics, facsimile images, voice and video message components)[8];
• X.500 electronic mail directories of group and organisational information[9] (though in their most comprehensive form such directories could act as key infrstructure components supporting all categories of CSCW systems);
• real time 'desktop video conferencing' systems incorporated into workstations and personal computers[8];
• large video wall screen systems (such as, a video link between two public places in different buildings so that people walking by 'bump into' one another; or the linking of two meeting rooms by providing each with a whole wall view of the other)[10].

Shared Work Space Systems

When people work together they often use existing documents, pads or whiteboards to draw or write things for mutual consumption. These are essentially shared work spaces, and the material created on them is often used as the basis for further discussion, and is annotated accordingly. Even when an individual's notes are not created for general consumption they sometimes form the basis of a subsequent contribution, verbal or otherwise from that person. Observations such as these have motivated CSCW researchers to investigate the role that shared work spaces play in group work, and to build tools which can support the process.

Examples of shared work space tools under development are:
- remote screen sharing facilities (whereby a part of an individual's screen is reproduced on one or more other screens, and special facilities enable the users of each screen to point to parts of the shared area or to make changes or annotations)[11];
- face-to-face meeting support using shared individual screens and large public screens[12][13];
- electronically aided, intelligent whiteboards which provide support for drawing, listing, collating, reorganising, inclusion into an electronic document or store, and printing out[14].

Shared Information Systems

People working together often start from a base of common information, and usually generate a quantity of shared information during the course of their work. Facilities are required to support the input, storage, navigation and retrieval of that information by all members of the group. The information may be in text, numeric, graphic, image or video form.

Examples of shared information facilities being developed are:
- multimedia, multi-user hypertext systems which enable information to be held in chunks, and for each chunk to be linked to other chunks. In this way a 'standard' route through the information can be provided. Individuals are also able to create their own routes, and to add information of their own (designated as either public or private material)[15][16];
- shared optical disc or CD-ROM systems which enable large numbers of documents, or other large volumes of information, to be made available to work groups;
- multi-user databases of a variety of types to support the sharing of textual and and numeric data among work groups[17].

Group Activity Support Systems

People who work together usually either know what they have to do and how they are going to do it, or they agree goals and procedures between themselves. Even when procedures are not formally agreed individuals constantly strive to establish 'next steps' and to ascertain their role in the group. This organisation and common understanding of the work process is an essential prerequisite to progress being made. Meeting this need is a three part process: first, goals must be established; second procedures must be established and agreed; and third, the procedures must be visible and carried out.

Examples of activity support tools being developed are:
- procedure processing or work flow systems enabling electronic forms to be sent on predefined routes of people and roles, collecting specified information and alternating routes according to the inputs made. Reminders and status reports can be automatically produced[18][5];
- activity processors which allow a more general form of work flow / procedure processing by not constraining input to forms, and by enabling more flexible, conversation-type interaction to be moderated by an activity 'script' for the participants[19];
- methodologies and support tools for groups to analyse, define and prototype the organisation, procedures and equipment with which they are to carry out a group activity[20][21];

- specialised coordination, procedure processing and activity processing systems to support the systems development process[22];
- co-authoring tools to support the joint writing of documents by two or more people[23];
- idea generation and prioritising tools to aid group creativity[24][13];
- decision support tools to display facts and options to groups and to help groups make decisions [24][7];
- argumentation tools to help the members of a group make their positions explicit and to understand the views of their colleagues[25];
- naming tools to help groups define their terminology as they proceed with the work[26].

5.2 Infrastructure Technologies

To implement each of the CSCW enabling technologies described in Section 5.1, a number of infrastructure technologies are required. Some of these are available today, others are not. The table below summarises the position in the early 1990s.

CSCW component	Infrastructure technologies available today	Infrastructure technologies not yet widely available
Communication Systems		
• Advanced electronic mail	- Local/wide area nets - High-resolution PCs	- High bandwidth networks - Voice/video input on PCs - X.400 infrastructure
• X.500 directory group information		- X.500 software products - Architecture to integrate X.500 into corporate and CSCW systems
• Desktop video conferencing		- High bandwidth networks - Voice/video input on PCs - Fast signal compression / decompression systems
• Large screen video wall systems		- High bandwidth networks - Voice/video input on PCs - High resolution wall screens - Fast signal compression / decompression systems
Shared Work Space Systems • Remote screen sharing	- Local/wide area nets	- High bandwidth networks
• Shared screens to support face-to-face meetings	- Back projection systems	- High resolution wall screens
• Intelligent whiteboards	- Touch screens - Pen input devices	- High resolution wall screens - Appropriate software

CSCW component	Infrastructure technologies available today	Infrastructure technologies not yet widely available
Shared Information Systems		
• Multi-user hypertext	- Local/wide area nets	- Distributed database software - Flexible multi-user functionality
• Shared optical disc systems	- Local/wide area nets - High resolution PCs - Scanning devices - Juke box systems - Search/retrieval software	- High bandwidth networks
• Multi-user databases	- Local/wide area nets	- Distributed database software - Flexible multi-user functionality
Group Activity Support Systems		
• Procedure processors	- Procedure processing software	- Seamless integration with electronic mail systems
• Activity processors / work flow systems	- Commitment making software	- General purpose, flexible, activity processing software - Seamless integration with electronic mail systems - Tools for defining activities
• Group work design tools		- Easy to use tools for each part of a coherent group work design process
• System development tools		- System developers workbench with integral group support tools
• Co-authoring tools	- Word processors	- Easy to use software to support all phases of the joint authoring process
• Idea generation/prioritising tools	- Appropriate software for face-to-face and distributed meetings	- Meeting rooms equipped with one or more PCs and a large wall screen - Appropriate software for asynchronous situations
• Decision support tools	- Appropriate software for face-to-face and distributed meetings.	- Meeting rooms equipped with one or more PCs and large wall screens. - Appropriate software for asynchronous situations
• Argumentation tools		- Appropriate software
• Naming tools		- Appropriate software integrated into a group support software environment

There is also a more general infrastructure requirement for effective CSCW work; that is for an open systems environment in which material from different systems (for example, from two different word processing systems) can be successfully exchanged without losing format or meaning in the process; and in which work can be coordinated across and within several different application programmes. Such a CSCW environment was not available at the beginning of the 1990s, although researchers were beginning to address the problem.

6 Group Process Aspects

Four categories of Group Process Aspects were identified in Chapter Three.
• individual aspects;
• organisational aspects;
• group work design aspects;
• group dynamics aspects.

These categories are not mutually exclusive - a particular CSCW implementation may well take account of some or all of these aspects, as well as any combination of the enabling technologies described in Chapter Five.

6.1 Individual Aspects

The characteristics, skills, knowledge and artefacts that individuals bring with them to the group working process have a crucial impact on the groups effectiveness. Consequently, considerable effort is being made to understand individual characteristics and their significance for the design of CSCW tools and group processes.

Work on individual aspects is being done in the following areas.

Human Communication Characteristics

• Human communication research is investigating the way humans talk to each other and use speech to make commitments and take action. This work builds on existing knowledge in the fields of linguistics, pragmatics, discourse analysis and speech act theory; and is producing new languages to specify group work[19], and new functionality to support group activities[27].

Individual Work Patterns

• The contributions that an individual makes to a group are almost always influenced by the working practices, styles and constraints of the individual concerned. Even when an alternative way of working is adopted, the individual's habits and predilections show through. These factors need to be understood and taken into account in the design of group support tools and working practices[28]. Among the most interesting contributions made in this area are those from an anthropological perspective[29]. A considerable amount of work has also been done on the patterns of use of electronic mail and computer conferencing systems[30].

Interface Design for Group Support Systems

• In the course of prototyping group support systems, researchers are constantly encountering challenges of how to represent information and provide novel facilities[31]. For example, in allowing all participants to share a common screen in an idea generation and prioritisation system, a mechanism has to be found for indicating that a particular piece of text or graphic is being manipulated by someone else and therefore not available for anyone else to work on. One answer to this problem was to 'grey out' the material concerned[13]. Such design solutions often depend on a combination of ingenuity and knowledge in fields such as human perception and cognitive psychology.

6.2 Organisational Aspects

Groups of any size have to be organised and managed if they are to be effective. This is just as true for small groups in, say, a face-to-face meeting as it is for large organisations (which are a particular manifestation of the group working process with their own macro-level problems and requirements). Areas in which CSCW research is investigating organisational issues are described below.

Representation of Organisational Knowledge

• Knowing how an organisation is structured, and who does what and how, is a prerequisite for most of its members to get things done. Yet there is often too much organisational information to find out about and remember. And, to add to the problem, organisational information changes frequently. Work addressing these issues includes investigations of the potential of X.500 directories as repositories for organisational information[9]; the inclusion of job descriptions and responsibilities in group activity support systems[32]; and the representation of organisational structures in graphical form[20].

Organisation Design

• The structure of organisations has been an issue of great interest to Management Science for many years[33]. Now, however, CSCW is beginning to address this question from a variety of different perspectives[34][35]. CSCW work in this area is still in its early stages so its long term direction is not clear. However, one development might be the provision of tools to support organisational change by integrating pre-specified goals together with knowledge about how groups and individuals work best.

Management Issues

• As CSCW research develops new support tools, new requirements appear for the management of activities, people and resources[36]. One example is the way in which two or more geographically separate people sharing a screen, need some kind of management facility to determine who has control of the screen and its functions. At a different level, managers of large organisations will need to know how to orchestrate their staff using advanced electronic mail and other group support systems; and how to develop effective cultures of group work within their organisations.

6.3 Group Work Design Aspects

Group work, like any other work, requires effective planning and organisation. This requires that work goals are identified and a work process designed. Conventional system design methods are not well suited to the combination of formal and informal activities undertaken in group work, so CSCW researchers are investigating a variety of alternative approaches.

User Involvement

• The people most likely to know and understand what goes on in informal group activities, and how they feel about the part they play in them, are the participants themselves. Therefore, they hold the key to building effective solutions for the activities concerned. Furthermore, people who have been involved in organising their own work usually have more positive attitudes and are keener to make the eventual solution work. Hence, much CSCW research is being done - particularly in the Scandinavian countries - to establish methods by which users can contribute to the design and evaluation process[37].

Prototyping and Usability Testing

- User involvement, however, is not enough to ensure success: human interaction within work groups is complex and unpredictable, so the possibility of designing badly is great. To ensure effective solutions, designs must be tried out under as near real-world working situations as possible, with user reactions being recorded, analysed and used to adjust the designs. Such techniques, first developed by the Human-Computer Interaction community, are being adapted and used in CSCW work[38][39].

Group Work Design Procedures

- There is a growing awareness of the need to provide clear guidelines for the analysis and design of CSCW solutions. This need will become all the more apparent as more flexible, user-configurable group working tools become available. The design procedures that are developed are likely to draw heavily on the User Involvement and Prototyping approaches described above, and will probably also take into account most of the other group process aspects described in this chapter[21][40].

6.4 Group Dynamics Aspects

Understanding the way individuals behave within groups, and the way groups perform, enables the most appropriate group support methods, procedures and computer tools to be devised. Important variables being considered in this work are group size (groups of 2 upwards), time span of collaboration (a few hours up to many years), and proximity (face-to-face, or remote collaboration via text mail, screen sharing, video links, etc.). CSCW work in this area is described below.

The Collaborative Process

- A number of CSCW researchers have been studying collaboration between pairs of individuals. This has identified some common characteristics such as the insight that most collaboration activity is either substantive (development of the topic in hand, annotative (questions, clarifications, elaborations, acceptance, etc.), or procedural (issues not related to the topic in hand, but how to address it)[16]. Such insights are of great value in contributing to the design of group work tools. Other works from sociological and anthropological perspectives are also making contributions to CSCW in this area[41].

Group Performance

- There has been considerable interest for many years in whether group performance is affected by different media such as computer conferencing systems and video conferencing, and a wealth of material on the subject has been published[42]. As newer technologies and CSCW functionality emerges, researchers continue to investigate the relative effectiveness of different media[43].

Group Behaviour

- Closely allied to the subject of group performance is the question of how individuals behave when they are in a group. Much work of this nature has been done by Social Psychologists. CSCW researchers are utilising this knowledge and building upon it - particularly by empirical studies of groups working in real-world non-laboratory conditions[44]; and in studies of groups using prototype CSCW tools[24].

7 The Impact of CSCW on Business and Government

Organisations, by their very nature, rely on people working together. Consequently, CSCW has the potential to make a dramatic impact on the activities of business and government. However, as most CSCW researchers emphasise, it is difficult to predict the overall impact since the field is still in its infancy. It will require extensive practical experience of the use of CSCW in organisations, both large and small, of varying degrees of complexity, before answers to these questions emerge. Instead, for the present, it is more productive to consider the impact of the components of the Enabling Technologies and Group Process Aspects identified in Chapters Five and Six. Section 7.1 below describes how each of these components might develop during the 1990s. Subsequent sections assess how those developments might affect business trends and the roles of various categories of staff - particularly the business of government and its employees.

In reading this chapter it should be remembered that the impact of CSCW is likely to evolve over several decades; and that the impact of the more advanced technologies will be highly dependent on the inter-relation between take-up and how quickly costs fall.

7.1 Timeline Analysis

This section assesses what the major developments are likely to be in each of the four main areas of CSCW technology - communication systems, shared workspaces, shared information systems and group activity support systems.

CSCW Communication System Developments

Five major factors are likely to have a significant impact on the development of communication systems over the next five years. Firstly, the growth in the number of installed and networked personal computers will increase the number of people who are accessible by electronic communication and who are experienced in using electronic communication facilities. Secondly, the establishment of national and international X.400 electronic mail capabilities will increase the use and usefulness of electronic mail. Thirdly, continued growth in the number of installed local area networks will introduce electronic mail, and the electronic mail culture, to more and more people. Fourthly, the introduction of ISDN could provide greater bandwidth and faster, cheaper and more reliable communications than are currently available. Lastly, increased bandwidth and improved compression algorithms will reduce the installation difficulties and cost of video conferencing.

Consequently, by the mid-1990s, the use of electronic mail will be much more widespread than it is now. Suppliers, businesses and government departments will be more aware of the need to invest in improved email facilities specifically to support group work.

It is less predictable how the video-based capabilities of CSCW technology will progress through this period. There will certainly be a rapid growth in understanding how video can be put to best use, and the range of functionality that should be provided with its delivery system. There will also be a wide range of products on the market to support video. However it is not yet clear if the price of using desktop video conferencing (price here includes end-user equipment costs and communication charges) will be low enough to generate a large market by the turn of the century.

Developments in Shared Work Space Systems

Shared workspace facilities are already widely available in one form or another and have attracted a significant base of users. Indeed, one article reviewing ICL's 'DeskTop Conferencing' product (combined voice communication and shared screen, via ISDN), speculated that this might even surpass the importance of desktop publishing[45]. Whether it will have quite so great an impact remains to be seen. However, it is not a particularly difficult or expensive technology to implement, so it is likely to be widely available and used by the mid-1990s. The Advanced Concepts Branch of CCTA has a shared workspace concept demonstrator featuring, among other things, facilities which support the process of document development by participants in different geographical locations.

The extension of the voice component of desktop conferencing to include on-screen video conferencing could be a particularly potent productivity tool in overcoming the problems caused by people working in geographically separated locations. Clearly, government departments and large businesses could make great use of such a facility. Desktop video conferencing technology will certainly be readily available by the end of the 1990s, but cost factors will play a key role in determining its take-up.

Developments in Shared Information Systems

Shared information facilities are already becoming an important feature of Local Area Networks. People are beginning to see the advantages of holding general information such as telephone directories, administrative information and procedure manuals within a network fileserver. As experience and use of these facilities grows, people will find a wider range of information which can be held centrally to serve the work group.

By the late 1990s there will be a much greater understanding of what information can usefully be held in local, departmental and corporate file servers and how it can be maintained and secured. Advances in database and storage technologies will support this trend towards shared information, and will enable image and voice information to be held in addition to text. However, such advances will be less critical than the development of organisational cultures, both inside and outside government, which understand the importance of group information, which are able to identify the information most important to organisational goals, and which can provide such information and maintain it effectively.

Developments in Group Activity Support Systems

It is likely that group activity support products will have a very significant impact during the rest of the decade. In the vanguard of this development are procedure processors and work flow systems which automate the paper-based forms-passing process. These are likely to come into widespread use in the next five to ten years because of the growing numbers of networked workstations, and because the concept is easy to understand and can be justified in terms of improved control and faster document turn-around times.

Other, more generalised, group support tools will also become available to assist the establishment, organisation and monitoring of work groups and their activities. Many such products will embody entirely new concepts so it is not yet possible to foresee what impact they will make. Many organisations will conduct pilot studies in the mid 1990s to identify tools which can help their work groups cope with an increasingly complex and fast-moving world. Specific application areas, such as the software development process, will pioneer these novel CSCW concepts. For example, it is probable that by the end of the 1990s, Integrated Programming Support Environments (IPSE's) will possess coordination and commitment making facilities to support the work of groups of programmers.

Developments in Meeting Room Facilities

Another notable development is the impact that the combination of enabling technologies will have on the meeting room of the future. This is an area in which detailed CSCW research is being done, with the aim of equipping meeting rooms with computers or terminals at each seat, and with large public screens and special meeting support software. Appropriate software will be available in the mid-1990s, though the expense of configurations will probably limit the number of fully equipped rooms that any one organisation could afford to install. However, many meeting rooms will undergo some less costly changes over the next decade. In particular, it is now feasible to hook an organisation's network to a computer in a meeting room, and to display corporate or departmental information by front or back projection techniques. It is feasible to use such a facility to take minutes or to work on texts during meetings, and to project visual aids created with presentation software.These working practices are likely to become increasingly common in the 1990s, both in the private sector and in large government departments.

Developments in the Individual Aspects of CSCW

Theoretical work on human communication is already starting to be applied in commitment and coordination products, and this trend from theory to practice will continue. The most recent research in this field will take several years to be applied, so it is probable that a succession of increasingly sophisticated commitment and coordination products will emerge over the next ten years.

There is a growing awareness of the need to cater for variations in the computing environment and for the differing individual skill levels. This will prompt CSCW developers to provide systems which can interwork and interchange data in different formats. The growth in use of portable personal computers may stimulate novel approaches to the equipping of meeting rooms. CSCW advances will stimulate new interface technologies and designs - particularly for voice and video applications - in the late 1990s.

Developments in the Organisational Aspects of CSCW

In the mid-1990s, current research on the storage of organisational information in (X.500) Directories will come to fruition. It will then be clearer what information can be held and what the maintenance overhead will be; though the eventual role of directory systems in corporate and departmental systems will take more time to emerge.

Research into the organisational impact of CSCW is growing, investigating such things as the responses of people to the introduction of CSCW technology, how they may cope with the increased information load that it could bring, and determining the requirements for implementation and training programmes. In addition, our understanding of the different ways in which group processes can and should be organised will grow, to the point where it is possible that guidelines for organising and managing groups may be provided within various CSCW products.

The growth of a national and international electronic mail culture is expected to gather pace in the late 1990s. Executives, managers, and government officers will become increasingly aware of the growing importance of electronic mail and other group support systems, will make greater use of autonomous teams and ad-hoc groups as the systems become more commonly used, and will become more skilled at managing people via such systems.

Developments in Group Work Design Methods

A major question which is central to the development of CSCW is how group work systems are to be designed and implemented. In the short term this will be answered by the use of ad-hoc procedures or modifications of existing IT methods. However, such approaches are unlikely to be able to take account of the informal qualities of group work and its dependence on the motivation of the individual. By the second half of the 1990s the need for a specialised CSCW method will have become apparent. Emerging CSCW methods will be provided in the form of computer-based toolsets, or as integral parts of CSCW activity support tools.

An example of work being done in government on the group working process is the development of Group Work Design Procedures by Dr John Bowers of Manchester University in collaboration with the Advanced Concepts Branch of CCTA [21]. This aims to specify clear procedures for the introduction of CSCW technology, where appropriate, based on the actual working patterns which people follow when they work in teams.

Developments in Group Dynamics Aspects

Many of the results of 1980s' research into the collaborative process will begin to be reflected in products around the mid-1990s. Further research on collaboration will provide a steady stream of inspiration for product enhancements in the late 1990s and beyond. Research into group performance in different media, and practical experience of different media in real work settings, will lead to greater planned use of a mix of media for group work. Training in how to behave when using different CSCW systems (such as desktop video conferencing) may be popular towards the end of the 1990s.

7.2 Analysis of Business and Government Needs

The following eight major business needs of any organisation for the 1990s were identified in Section 3.5:
• improved communication between people;
• reduction in the time needed to make decisions;
• improvement in the timeliness and quality of strategic decisions;
• ability to make rapid changes in organisation structure;
• ability to move faster into new markets;
• ability to change and create products faster;
• reduced teamwork overheads and improved teamwork performance
• improved levels and quality of service.

CSCW's potential impact on these business needs is described below.

Impact on Improving Communications

Communication by electronic mail, as already discussed in Section 7.1, will become more widespread in the 1990s. This will have two effects on the speed of communication within and between groups: firstly, communication between individuals will be more immediate; and secondly, fewer groups will be slowed down by the inability of just a few members to communicate electronically. In addition, the growth in portable computer usage will reduce communication delays when people are travelling or at home.

The impact of multiparty desktop video conferencing capabilities is much harder to predict, but, in principle at least, they could make it considerably easier to arrange and conduct meetings in a shorter timeframe. Certainly, if businesses or government departments want to speed up their communications, CSCW technology will provide them with increasingly effective solutions for many years to come. The key to achieving such improvements, however, will lie in motivating individuals to use the technology, in proving its relevance and efficacy, and in building corporate and governmental cultures which will take advantage of it.

Impact on the Time Needed to Make Decisions

Decision making involves several distinct sub-processes including acquiring information, assessing it, considering options, discussing them with colleagues, simulating solutions, establishing advantages and disadvantages, and making a case for management to consider. Large, complex decision-making processes can often take weeks or months, and may demand an inordinate amount of effort by employees. Hence there is a widespread desire to reduce the time taken to make decisions so that organisations can be more responsive and so that the resulting benefits can be achieved faster. CSCW will contribute to this goal in a number of ways: improved communication facilities will help in a general sense, while brainstorming tools, argumentation tools, specially-equipped meeting rooms, and procedure and activity processors will all contribute to a more efficient decision making process. Of course, the availability of such tools only provides *the means* for speeding up decision making: to actually make things happen faster will also require clear management goal setting and direction, as well as control over the quantity and relevance of information that is used.

Impact on the Quality of Strategic Decisions

The quality of decisions depends on decision makers having an understanding of the objectives, on having all the relevant information, on being able to assess all the options, on being able to have consultations with relevant colleagues, and finally on choosing the best option. CSCW will contribute to the process by reducing the time and effort involved in a number of these stages, thereby enabling a more thorough job to be done. In particular, shared databases will make information more readily accessible; and improved communications and support for groups will make it easier to consult colleagues and discuss options.

Impact on Ability to Change Organisation Structures

When an organisation changes, its members need to be informed of the changes, of how they will be affected and of the implementation schedule. Versatile communications will aid this process. So, for example, CSCW holds out the prospect of managers being able to make announcements to all their staff, in multiple locations, via desktop video links. Shared databases of organisational information may make it easier for staff to find out the details of organisational changes. Activity tools specifying group activities by role will make it easy for staff to switch from one role to another. CSCW systems which reduce the need for co-workers to be co-located will ease the constraints of physical location on organisational structures.

Impact on Ability to Move into New Markets and Address New Needs

If a group or organisation wishes to move into new markets or address new departmental needs, information is required about what market opportunities exist and which new needs have emerged. Decisions then have to be made about which markets to enter or which needs to serve, plans drawn up and infrastructures established to serve the initiative. Shared databases make it feasible for all employees - not just sales, marketing and liaison staff - to record informal knowledge and information about market activities and opportunities, and new departmental requirements. Such devices turn the whole of the workforce into market researchers, gleaning information from such diverse sources as conversations, newspapers, magazines, TV, personal contacts, parliamentary reports or even personal consumer experiences.

The establishment of infrastructures for new markets and needs will be greatly facilitated by CSCW's improved communications; and by the ability to design and support new work processes quickly and with reduced dependence on the physical location of those involved.

Impact on the Speed of Creating New Products

The creation of new products is highly dependent on effective collaboration between researchers, product developers, marketing staff, manufacturers and distributors. To address departmental needs effectively it must also be possible for government officers, both generalists and specialists, inter-departmental liaison staff, and perhaps manufacturers or distributors of relevant products to, collaborate effectively. CSCW's wide range of collaboration support tools could have a major effect on the product creation process - provided that organisation cultures do not prevent the different groups from working in concert. Of key importance here will be the various informal group communication mechanisms, such as computer conferencing systems, that can support ongoing communication. Activity support tools which can formalise the relationships between the groups and roles involved in the product creation process, will also have an important part to play.

Impact on Teamwork Effectiveness

CSCW will have a direct impact on the effectiveness of teams. The extent of its success will depend on the ability of an organisation to focus on the goals it wants to achieve, and on its ability to implement appropriate CSCW tools and motivate its staff to use them. Organisations will also have to ensure that a suitable computer infrastructure is in place: individuals will need their own (portable) computers, configured to provide free and easy access to appropriate communication networks and information resources, and must be trained so that they can work with appropriate media and software.

Impact on Quality of Service

Organisations should be able respond to the needs of customers and clients efficiently and effectively, and to sort out their problems quickly and courteously. CSCW can help meet these requirements in a number of ways: firstly, shared information databases can hold details of contacts between any of the organisation's employees and any of its customers, thus overcoming the problem of the one hand not knowing what the other is doing. If this information is responsibly shared between employees then it can lead to better coordination within an organisation. Secondly, improved internal communications will enable government departments or suppliers to provide a single point of contact for customers while still providing fast and effective responses to queries. Improved internal communications and activity support tools will enable customer problems to be sorted out quickly, and will reduce the likelihood of problems arising in the first place.

7.3 Function Analysis

This section discusses the impact of CSCW on the following categories of employees: executives and managers; professionals; technicians; secretarial and support personnel; clerical workers and manual workers.

Impacts on Executives and Managers

Executives and managers work in two sorts of groups - in groups of their peers with whom they must operate as a team to ensure the success of the enterprise, and in groups of those whom they are directing and managing. CSCW could have a significant impact on both these aspects of the jobs of managers - if they are prepared to use the technology. Currently, however, a significant proportion of managers do not yet use a computer as in integral part of their day-to-day work. Three of the most prevalent reasons for this are:

- many managers or government officers simply do not see the need for such a tool in their managerial activities;
- a significant change in working practices is required to use them;
- a significant amount of time and effort are needed to acquire the necessary skills to use a personal computer and its applications.

Although many of today's managers and executives may never surmount these problems, the number of such people with computing skills *will* grow as time goes by, not least because younger staff with personal experience of using their own computers will eventually rise to these positions.

Improved communication facilities will be of particular interest to executives and managers - particularly the easy accessibility of desktop video conferencing (DVC). It is possible that the late 1990s will see a sizeable number of management staff using DVC as an integral part of their daily work.

An increasing number of senior managers and government officers are likely to have access to advanced meeting rooms by the late 1990s, to support the use of Executive Information Systems in management meetings. CSCW software tools to aid the meeting and decision-making process may be incorporated into such facilities as they become available. In fact, teams of managers who use computers extensively in their work may go further and equip their meeting rooms with computers (or laptop connection points) at each position, a large shared electronic whiteboard, and a full range of multi-participant interactive meeting room software.

Throughout the 1990s managers in both private and public sectors, will become increasingly aware of the importance of central stores of information and will organise the establishment and maintenance of such stores. Their use will often involve looking at multiple sources of information in different windows on their computer workstation screens, cutting and pasting text, data and graphics as appropriate, and integrating the pieces to produce the answers, summaries or business cases they require. Some of the information will originate in the corporate or departmental data processing systems and some in external databases. The remainder, however, will be information acquired and maintained by employees in the course of their jobs: sales leads, information about competitors, new product information, business trends, customer requirements, new departmental requirements, employee interests and skills, etc.

Managers will become increasingly skilled at identifying the information they need, at organising the establishment and maintenance of such databases, and at using the information to analyse situations and take initiatives. In addition, the functional power of CSCW tools such as multimedia hypertext will be improved to support information storage requirements.

Group activity support tools offer a rich set of facilities for managers to organise and control their departmental operations and procedures more effectively. Procedure processors and work flow systems will become increasingly popular tools, while a variety of software products to support group or departmental activities such as idea generation, planning, analysis of different viewpoints, commitment making, and team organisation, will become available. Developments such as these will reinforce the move towards localised computing operations supported by corporate data processing, networking and database facilities.

| Impacts on Professionals | In some respects the jobs of professional specialists resemble those of managers: professionals often work in teams with their peers, they have authority and responsibilities, and they often direct other employees. Therefore, much of what has already been said about managers also applies to professionals. Certainly they, like managers, will make use of advanced communication capabilities, such as desktop conferencing and desktop video conferencing, when they become commonly available. |

Professionals, however, are also specialists and will increasingly be using specialised computer packages and facilities to support their work. For example, doctors are using diagnostic support packages, architects are using computer-aided design systems, and accountants are using specialised spreadsheet configurations. while working with their peers, professionals will need communication systems that can cope with the transport and reconstitution of such specialised information, and CSCW systems will be designed to meet that requirement.

The nature of a professional job often demands problem-solving, creativity and innovation. Therefore advanced meeting rooms equipped with software to support creativity and problem-solving will be of great interest to this category of employee. Work of this kind will also be done in individual offices with the software running on a workstation and the participants gathered round the desk. If the price of large size flat screens falls sufficiently, some may be installed in offices to facilitate this sort of ad-hoc activity.

Another aspect of professional life is the need to keep up to date with the subject, to maintain external contacts and to belong to independent professional associations. Hence, professionals may benefit from the ability to access remote systems which provide information and communication services for their profession.

Some professionals may also make use of shared databases to learn from each other's experiences. Activity support tools will be used by many professionals to support collaborative working processes with peers or colleagues. Such processes, currently undertaken mainly through paper, will increasingly be carried out using procedure processors, work flow systems or coordination software.

Impacts on Technicians

Technicians are trained primarily for practical work in a specialised area. They tend to have less executive authority and responsibility than professionals. Furthermore, their job content tends to be narrower and they usually do less work in groups. Hence, their need for CSCW tools is correspondingly less. However, in tackling practical problems, they do need to accumulate a vast amount of knowledge about how things work, what can go wrong and why, and how practical problems can be overcome. CSCW tools such as shared databases and computer conferencing systems will enable the knowledge and experiences of each technician to be shared, and the combined resources of the technician workforce to be brought to bear on each problem. Technicians will also use communication systems to talk to their managers and professional colleagues, and to the organisation's secretaries and support staff.

Impacts on Secretarial and Administrative Workers

Secretaries and administrative support personnel provide assistance to others and consequently will make considerable use of CSCW tools to work with the people they are supporting. Communication systems will be heavily used by this group of staff. Activity support tools such as procedure processors and activity processors will assist them in their administrative operations. Secretaries and support personnel being given additional responsibilities in the future for organising and maintaining shared databases.

Impacts on Clerical Staff

The traditional paper-management role of clerical workers has been changing for some time, and the introduction of CSCW tools will continue this process. In particular, procedure processors, work flow systems and activity processors will automate many of the tasks relating to paper forms, thereby eliminating much of the manual activity of sorting, filing and retrieving paper. Clerical staff will make considerable use of communication systems both to carry out their functional tasks and to communicate with their fellow clerical workers and with their management.

Impacts on Manual Workers

Most organisations have manual workers of one sort or another, but they are not normally expected to have regular access to the sort of computing infrastructure required by CSCW. However, this group is discussed here for two reasons. First, as organisational communications become more electronically-based, this group of workers may become isolated. Will this be a problem - particularly if current trends to reduce divisions within organisations continue? Second, the trend towards involving production line workers in identifying problems and improving the production process is likely to continue, and could become a widespread practice by the end of the decade - but will it still be based on face-to-face meetings with no computer support? Answers to these two questions will not become clear for many years. In the meantime, organisations would do well to monitor the morale and attitudes of their manual workforce as CSCW systems become the mainstay of communication and activity among the rest of their employees.

Impacts on all Workers: Company Communications and Training

Two CSCW applications are likely to have an impact on all workers. The first - company communications - follows naturally from the uses each category of worker will make of advanced communication systems. By the turn of the century, electronic mail cultures will be prevalent in most organisations, and desktop video conferencing will be starting to become popular. These are likely to develop into an organisation's primary means of communication, whether that organisation be in the private or public sector. Large wall screen displays can assist this process by enabling public messages to be broadcast to those who are not in the proximity of a workstation.

The second CSCW application likely to impact all workers lies in the area of training. Tutored learning, possibly done in groups, via a combination of real time face-to-face sessions and activity processor work spread over weeks or months, will be facilitated by the introduction of CSCW techniques. Participants in such sessions - students and tutors alike - will not have to be co-located, and experts may be brought in to contribute at appropriate points in the courses. The widespread emergence of such distance training depends on when advanced communication facilities come into widespread use - probably around the end of the 1990s.

In Summary...

Given the business needs and communication demands of organisations in the 1990s, it is highly likely that CSCW techniques will be introduced over an increasing range of activities in the next few years. In particular, government departments, given their size, complexity, and dispersal, and given the development of the customer-responsive philosophy, will find an increasing need for efficient teamwork and for CSCW technologies which can develop and support solutions to these needs.

8 CSCW Benefits and Risks

Many of the benefits and risks of implementing CSCW concepts and systems will have become apparent in Chapter Seven. Rather than cover the same ground again, summaries are provided in the tables below. No attempt has been made to consider cost in this chapter because they will vary depending on the products used, the applications concerned and the approach that is taken. Also, costs are falling and will continue to do so for several years. However readers should remember that, when implementing a CSCW system, the benefits must be weighed against both risks and costs.

8.1 Benefits and Risks of CSCW Components

CSCW Component	Benefits of CSCW	Risks of CSCW
CSCW communication systems	• Interworking with others will be easier • Work will not be so constrained by travel problems	• Some people may not work as well in a particular medium • Cost may limit certain channels to certain classes of employee • Misuse of video facilities could invade people's privacy
Shared work space systems	• Substantive work can be done with remote people in real time	• Lack of standards may restrict facility to similar systems
Shared information systems	• Knowledge possessed by the workforce can be shared • Organisations will be able to act in a more coordinated fashion	• Could lose competitive edge if shared databases got into wrong hands • Information input by staff may vary in reliability • Volume of information may make it difficult to access
Group activity support systems	• Activity status easier to monitor • Ad-hoc activities more likely to be done effectively and on time • Less paper to organise and file	• A proliferation of ad-hoc automated procedures may be difficult to control
Face-to-face meeting rooms	• Meetings can be shorter and more productive • All relevant information can be displayed to meeting members	• Unskilled staff may be unable to make effective use of facilities • Expensive investments may be under-utilised
Individual aspects	• Systems will become more attune to human characteristics	• Theoretical findings may result in impractical facilities
Organisational aspects	• Smaller, more autonomous teams can take more initiatives • People, roles and job functions will be easier to find out about	• Organisational information may be difficult to change resulting in inflexibility • More distributed organisations may be more difficult to control
Group work design aspects	• The process of applying CSCW will become easier and quicker	• Procedures for designing group work may be too long-winded and difficult to apply
Group dynamics aspects	• Group working support tools will incorporate functionality in tune with human characteristics	• Individuality and spontaneity may be constrained by standard software and approaches

8.2 CSCW Benefits and risks with respect to business needs

Business goals	Benefits of CSCW	Risks of CSCW
Improved communication	• Communication between individuals will be easier / faster • It will be easier to keep in touch with group members who travel • Meeting organisation will be less dependent on getting people together in one room	• People without access to specific communication systems may get excluded from groups • Faster pace of business life will put more stress on individuals • More time spent communicating may mean less time for thinking and other work
Reduced time to make decisions	• Communication systems/activity processors can speed up parts of the decision making process	• Ease of communication may mean more people want to be involved thereby increasing the time for decisions to be made
Improved quality of decisions	• Shared databases may facilitate more informed decisions • CSCW tools will support creativity and innovation in identifying solutions • CSCW tools will enable more people to contribute opinions and comments	• CSCW tools may prompt more effort than appropriate in particular decision making processes
Greater ability to change organisation structures	• Physical location of employees may be less of a constraint on organisation stuctures • Procedure and activity processors will make it easier to switch tasks between roles	• More organisation changes may be more stressful for staff • People who change jobs quickly will have less knowledge about the job
Faster movement into new markets	• Shared databases can enable the whole workforce to contribute market knowledge and ideas • Faster communication and the ability to devise automated support procedures fast, will facilitate faster moves into new markets	• Information in shared databases may be of variable reliability
Ability to change and create products faster	• CSCW tools can improve trust, interaction and collaboration between all groups involved in product development • Activity support tools may make product development more efficient, reliable, manageable	• Product quality may be sacrificed for speed of development
Improved teamwork performance	• CSCW tools can enable teams to organise their work better • Expertise and best practice embedded in CSCW tools can reduce dependence on a leader's skills and knowledge • Improved communications may make it easier to recruit appropriate team members	• Teams may spend too much time using CSCW tools and not concentrate enough on getting results • Creativity, innovation and discretion may be reduced if teams are subservient to standard CSCW tools and approaches

Business goals	Benefits of CSCW	Risks of CSCW
Improved quality of customer service	• Shared databases and improved communications make it possible for companies to have a unified view of relations with their customers • Improved communications can enable customer queries to be dealt with faster	• The customer may not have a unified view of his organisation's dealings with the supplier • Information in a shared customer database may be of variable reliability and open to different interpretations

8.3 Benefits and Risks of CSCW with Respect to Job Functions

Job function	Benefits of CSCW	Risks of CSCW
Executives and managers	• Communications with colleagues and staff will be easier and faster • Shared databases can enable managers to have their staff obtain and maintain the information they need • Procedure/activity processors enable managers to establish greater control over activities they are responsible for • Relevant information can be accessed and displayed during management meetings • Distance learning courses will be easier to undertake	• Managers who are unable to adapt to CSCW tools may feel isolated and threatened • Face-to-face meetings with staff may be reduced if managers rely too heavily on communication systems • Managers who are not skilled at working with CSCW tools may be less attractive to potential employers
Professionals	• Communication with colleagues will be easier and faster • CSCW systems may be able to transport specialised data and to reconstitute it at the other end • CSCW tools will support improved creativity, innovation and problem solving • The latest technical information will be easier to access • Professional opinions and experiences may be easier to exchange with other members of the same profession • Activity/procedure processors may reduce paperwork • Distance learning courses will be easier to undertake	• More time spent on communicating and keeping up to date may mean less time for thinking and other work • Improved external communications may increase the risk of inadvertently giving critical information to a competitor • Professionals who are not familiar with CSCW tools may be less attractive to potential employers

Job function	Benefits of CSCW	Risks of CSCW
Technicians	• Experiences will be easier to share with colleagues • Solutions to problems and challenges may be easier to establish from shared databases • Distance learning courses will be easier to undertake	• The time spent using CSCW tools may be more than the time saved by being able to solve problems faster
Secretaries and administrative support personnel	• Improved communications may ease making arrangements, organising meetings, etc. • The amount of paperwork to deal with and file may be less • Activity / procedure processors may reduce the amount of chasing and follow up work • Organising/maintaining shared databases may add interest and responsibility to the job • Distance learning courses will be easier to undertake	• If not everyone is using CSCW tools, work may have to be done twice - first in the CSCW system, and then again in an alternative medium
Clerical workers	• The amount of paperwork to deal with and file may be reduced • Activity /procedure processors will make it easier to establish the status of work in progress • Distance learning courses will be easier to undertake	• Activity and procedure processors may make it more difficult to arrange work-arounds with colleagues to deal with unusual circumstances • Activity and procedure processors may reduce the overall need for clerical staff
Manual workers	• Manual workers provided with access to communication systems may become more integrated with the organisation and more aligned with its goals	• Manual workers may become more isolated from the rest of the organisation

8.4 Other Benefits

The implementation of CSCW concepts and technology also has the potential to provide the following additional benefits.

Cross Organisation Interworking

In many large organisations it is difficult enough to find like-minded people let alone undertake some constructive work with them. CSCW holds out the prospect of supporting both these activities. Informal communication systems such as computer conferencing provide a means of identifying people with similar interests; and tools such as activity processors enable work to be planned and undertaken as a background activity.

More Opportunities for Initiative Takers

Cross-organisation activity is likely to be undertaken mainly by initiative takers - people who see opportunities or want to resolve problems, but cannot get much done on their own or in their own departments. Contemporary organisation structures tend to provide few opportunities for such people to act. CSCW tools, however, have the potential to release their creativity and potential.

More Ideas Expressed and Followed Up	It is the ability to undertake initiatives in the background, while still undertaking one's normal job, that is one of the primary benefits that CSCW offers. With this capability a great many more concepts and ideas can be openly expressed and discussed. Whereas in the past many good ideas may have simply been forgotten because of lack of time or difficulties in arranging action, CSCW tools may make it much easier to follow them through.

8.5 Other Risks

The implementation of CSCW concepts and technology may bring with it the following additional risks.

Information and Communication Overload

The combined impact of more communication, more information services and more shared databases could inflict serious overload on many staff. In the past it was difficult to obtain information and to communicate - people always wanted more than they could get. However, the tide is slowly turning: junk hardcopy mail is prevalent, and it is not uncommon to find people who have to spend at least half an hour each day dealing with their electronic mail. These phenomena should warn us to the dangers that could lie ahead. It is essential that CSCW solutions take into account the capabilities and time limitations of their human users.

Greater Reliance on Computer- Skilled Staff

Given the overload pressures, and the learning challenges of CSCW systems, it is not surprising that some employees will fare better than others. These will be the CSCW literate who may be in somewhat short supply in the years following the 1990s. To resolve this problem employers will have to provide appropriate training for their staff.

Greater Reliance on Computer Systems

The more use that is made of CSCW systems, the more organisations will come to rely and depend on them, so adequate provision must be made for failures. It would be unwise to assume that informal systems are any less important than formal DP systems in this respect - bear in mind the upset that occurs when the telephone system goes down for more than a few minutes.

Invasion of Privacy

There is a concern that, with so much communication and group activity going on via computer systems, it may be possible for other people - including management - to find out and monitor what individuals are doing. This fear does have some substance - but probably does not merit any greater concern than should be expressed about behaviour in the paper-based office. Basically, if someone wants to invade another's privacy in any type of media, then, provided they are determined and skilled enough, they will probably manage it. Naturally, all sensible precautions need to be taken, but CSCW systems can be as vulnerable, and as secure, as any other.

In fact, because CSCW functionality is being derived from a detailed understanding of the human condition, such problems have already been identified and solutions are being researched. However, to ensure that developments are not obstructed by data protection legislation, trade union concern, etc., supplier and user organisations should ensure that this issue is taken seriously and dealt with effectively.

9 Obtaining the Benefits

Throughout this volume it has been emphasised that the goal of CSCW is to improve the effectiveness of group working, and that CSCW solutions will draw on a range of resources including analysis and design methods, group organisation principles and computer-based support tools. It follows, therefore, that obtaining benefits from CSCW involves more than just installing software. Instead, organisations must familiarise themselves with CSCW philosophies, concepts and technologies; and then consider how CSCW can contribute towards their long-term business objectives.

9.1 Short-term Initiatives

Reading this volume and some of the relevant literature listed in Appendix E is a useful start; however, there is no substitute for practical experience, and the obvious place to get that is with a real work group problem or challenge somewhere in your organisation. It does not matter if the work group concerned is within your own department or branch - the key thing is that there should be a real business need to work on.

For example, perhaps there is some product or trend information which a group needs to maintain: a shared database might support this task. Perhaps the members of a work group travel too much to be able to sit down together and discuss experiences and strategy - maybe a computer conferencing system could help. Perhaps some geographically separated staff need to work simultaneously on the same text or spreadsheet: a screen sharing solution might be the answer. Or perhaps a major part of a group's activity is document creation: in this case a co-authoring system might be useful. Those are just a few examples - no doubt there are other group activities in your organisation which could be augmented.

It is not the aim of this report to explain in detail how to investigate and design CSCW solutions. Indeed, CSCW design procedures (such as that being developed by CCTA's Advanced Concepts Branch [21]) have yet to emerge. However, the CSCW literature indicates the general approaches to take. In particular you should:
- involve the work group in the analysis and design process, and ensure that the many informal aspects of their interworking relationships are identified and catered for;
- concentrate on understanding what the group perceives the fundamental business problems and needs are, based on their experience of the job;
- ensure that the solutions meet fundamental business needs and that the group is not being asked to do things just for the sake of an organisational arrangement, a standard reporting structure, or the constraints of computer technology or existing systems.
- try things out using rough and ready physical mock-ups, software prototypes and simulated work environments; plan to go round the design, build, test, redesign cycle several times; concentrate on practical usability testing in simulated work settings rather than critical commentary on paper proposals;

- design all aspects of the solution - computer support, face-to-face meetings, paper documents, job responsibilities, building layouts, workplace design - in an integrated fashion;
- design solutions encouraging collaboration and cooperation;
- don't be afraid to use your existing application systems and equipment but, where possible, do try out some of the newer systems and products identified in Section 3.6 and Appendix A;
- evaluate the group's activity and the opinions of its members BOTH before and after the pilot study: without 'before' data it is difficult to be objective.

After finishing a pilot study, write a report on what has happened, reviewing the problems and successes, and identifying future initiatives and suggested approaches. Involve the pilot work group in this exercise - by that time they will have plenty to contribute.

9.2 Long term goals

After completing the initial pilot work, CSCW developments can be tracked and CSCW-related initiatives which are clearly aligned to business needs can be proposed. Long term CSCW strategies can be developed and presented to IS/IT steering committees for inclusion in the organisation's overall information systems strategy. Strategies that may be appropriate for the organisation's CSCW work include:

- to create a networking infrastructure able to support text, image and voice, and providing communication systems such as electronic mail, computer conferencing, screen sharing, and video conferencing;
- to provide employees with equipment and facilities which enable them to stay in touch with their colleagues and work groups when they are away on business or at home;
- to upgrade meeting rooms so that information from the corporate network or an individual's machine can be displayed on a large screen in the meeting room;
- to train managers and other staff in techniques and computer tools for establishing, controlling and maintaining work groups;
- to institute methods that enable the experiences, opinions and requirements of individual group work participants to be investigated and taken into account, to a greater extent than is the practice in current approaches to computer system design;
- to create an environment in which groups are encouraged and able to contribute to the design of CSCW systems they are to use;
- to ensure that greater emphasis is given to usability testing of physical mock-ups and software prototypes, within multiple design, test, redesign cycles;
- to provide groups and individuals with greater autonomy, responsibility and freedom to act; and to encourage a climate of collaboration and initiative taking.

9.3 Further Advice on Obtaining CSCW Benefits

This chapter has provided initial guidance on what organisations can do to gain benefits from CSCW. However, during the first half of the 1990s CCTA's Advanced Concepts Branch will be conducting pilot experiments and evaluation work, to gain a more detailed understanding of how CSCW can be used to achieve business benefits. The results of this work will be published as they emerge, and a more definitive guide issued at the end of the evaluation period.

Appendix A   Short Descriptions of Some Products

The purpose of this appendix is to give readers a clearer view of the types of CSCW-related products that are commercially available. It is not intended to be a product directory or product listing. Items included have been randomly selected, and inclusion or exclusion from this appendix implies nothing. Readers requiring complete, up to date CSCW product listings may contact the CCTA Advanced Concepts Branch or CSC Europe.

A short description of at least one product in each category is given below. Categories are shown in the margin of each page, and a description of each category can be found in Section 3.6 of this volume.

Electronic Mail Systems

- **Telecom Gold from BT**: A publicly available service which can be accessed via dial up telephone lines (using a computer and modem) or by the Packet Switched Network. People rent an electronic mailbox and are provided with a username. Telecom Gold has related email services in many other locations worldwide. It also provides access to external information sources such as World Reporter and Jordans[46].

- **The Coordinator from Action Technologies Inc**: An email system running on PC compatible equipment and on networks such as Novell's Netware. A Novell brochure says of The Coordinator : "But electronic mail is only one of the functions The Coordinator performs. True, you can send mail even entire files, via The Coordinator to any connection in the world. But these messages can be requests for action, statements of possibilities to be discussed, assessments of situations, and conclusions to important dialogues. The Coordinator tracks these communications and gives you a complete record of all your conversations, commitments and transactions....On top of that The Coordinator shows you your goals and commitments on a daily, weekly, monthly, and yearly basis.".

- **QuickMail from CE Software**: An email system running on Macintosh computers. Messages can be sorted by priority, subject, recipient, or date; folders can be created for local storage. Sixteen files can be enclosed per message. Each user can establish a personal Mail Log to keep track of messages and can unsend and unread messages. Users can customise forms. Voicemail is supported, as is real-time conferencing[47].

Computer Conferencing Systems

- **VaxNotes from Digital Equipment Corporation (DEC)**: VaxNotes is bundled in with many DEC sales and is the computer conferencing system with the largest installed base. It is fully integrated with DEC's mail system and can operate over DECnet to permit users at any location to access a conference on another host[48].

- **Confer from Advertel Communication Systems Inc**: Confer is an IBM 370 based system which Advertel also offer as a timeshare system. A new VMS version has recently been announced. A UK Training Agency report described Confer as a simple 'two-dimensional' system where each conference contains a number of items and each item contains a number of responses. Additional facilities include the concept of an Auditor who can read but not write and Bulletins which are seen by conference members only once[48].

- **Caucus from Metasystems Design Group Inc**: Caucus is structured in a similar way to Confer and has many similar commands. However, it is available for a wider range of operating systems, including MS-DOS and Unix, which make it attractive to organisations who wish to start small and move to larger systems as they grow. Caucus is very easily extended and customised: all the textual prompts are held in a plain ASCII file. As a result several foreign langauge versions are available. The ease with which external routines can be linked into Caucus without access to source code, has resulted in a strong line of Third Party products including a range of menu systems, accounting and management packages and multi-site support facilities[48].

- **Compulink Information Exchange (CIX) from Compulink**: CIX is a commercial bulletin board and email service in the UK. It provides several hundred different conferences on a wide range of general interest and professional topics. In addition a 'Binmail' error correction service enables users to send complex messages and program files (a software patch to an application program, for example)[46].

Procedure Processing/work flow Systems

- **Staffware from FCMC**: Staffware is a Procedure Processor or work flow system designed to automate activities currently performed via paper-based forms. Staffware breaks a procedure into its component steps and enables a screen-based form to be designed complete with its addressees, deadlines and follow-on actions for each step. Staffware is distributed by OEMS such as Unisys and ICL - who have integrated it into their respective OFIS and OFFICEPOWER Office Automation systems.

Calendar Systems

- **Network Scheduler from Powercore Inc**: Network Scheduler provides personal event scheduling, meeting arrangement, letter writing and name and address filing facilities. It runs under the MS-DOS operating system and integrates with popular email packages. The Time Manager function informs users of tentative meeting arrangements by making the appropriate date blink. Individuals can then display the meeting information and press C to confirm or D to decline. Privacy levels can be set from 0-9 and dictate who can make changes to arranged appointments. The Appointment Book function allows individuals to view, list and update their own scheduled events; and the Calendar function gives an overview of the entire month and a graphic display of daily schedules[49].

Shared Filing Systems

- **IDEX from Office Workstations Limited**: IDEX is based on Office Workstation's Guide hypertext product. Guide enables users to create new documents and link existing ones together through the use of textual and graphic buttons interspersed throughout the text. The buttons also enable text within a document to be linked together. So, when reading a Guide document there is no need to read sequentially from start to finish; instead users can go where their interest lies by simply selecting the appropriate buttons. IDEX is essentially a multi-user version of Guide designed specifically to support department work groups that use large scale structured documentation. IDEX provides three levels of functionality: a System Manager can establish document types and templates (based on the Standard Generalized Markup Language, SGML); for Readers, content lists, help files and Boolean search facilities support the accessing of information within documents; and for Authors there are a range of document formatting tools.

- **Notes from Lotus Development Inc**: Rather than an application with a single focus, its a broad ranging tool with a variety of capabilities including shared databases, electronic mail, procedure processing and computer conferencing. "Notes' data structure is a cross between a table-oriented database and an outline. Each Notes database is a separate collection of documents which are generally created when a user fills in a form. This form can be as unstructured as a comment field with a title or as structured as a Roladex card. Forms can also can also be used for queries, as can 'views', which are akin to database reports. Views generally display a listing of documents, with or without details, with headings and column entries showing data in specified fields... Data can be sorted by any standard user-specified category, such as customer, person responsible (for a set of tasks or customer), date, problem, type etc... Data from different kinds of forms can be combined in a database or view, and different kinds of information can be associated with a particular customer"[17].

Co-authoring Systems

- **ForComment from Broderbund Software Inc**: ForComment is a document editing package that allows multiple reviewers to comment on a document, seeing and adding to each other's remarks without altering the original version. Only the designated author can choose to incorporate someone else's comments into the document. Context-sensitive help is provided and a 'cover page' tracks reviewers activities. ForComment is compatible with most word processing packages. It can be used by passing a disc round a group of users, but works much better if used in a networked environment[50].

Screen Sharing Systems

- **Timbuktu from Farallon**: Timbuktu is a Macintosh product enabling a user in one location to observe and control the screen activity of two or more remote Macintoshes and to transfer files between them. The remote screens are shown in separate resizable windows, while the user has full access to the local desktop and applications. 'Guests' to a machine are designated as either observers or controllers, and a pull down menu shows who is logged onto their machines in the network[51].

- **DeskTop Conferencing from ICL:** DeskTop Conferencing (DTC) allows two to eight people to participate in conference calls with simultaneous voice and data communications. Individuals can have control of the keyboard and can update everyone's screen simultaneously. All kinds of applications can be used during a conference call including spreadsheets, graphics and drawing programs. A variety of input devices can also be used including a light pen (to sign electronic signatures if so desired). DTC uses the Integrated Services Digital Network (ISDN) - the new digital telephone system being introduced in the UK and other countries. Each user requires a PC-compatible computer running the OS/2 operating system and a DTC package consisting of an ISDN telephone, an expansion card and conferencing software. Alternatively ICL can provide a preconfigured ISDN workstation[45]. A DOS Windows 3 version is also available.

Integrated Group Support Packages

- **Higgins from Enable Inc:** "Higgins is a well established Groupware product that offers very good electronic mail facilities along with a host of mini applications. Included are an editor, calendar, scheduler, calculator and call manager"[52]. Higgins also provides appointment handling, meeting arrangement and room booking facilities.

- **Into from ShareData Inc:** Into is described as a 'total office automation system'. It includes a word processor, spreadsheet, graphics facility, database, appointment book, electronic mail, office scheduler, and telephone book. The Office Scheduler will find the first available time for a meeting and will notify the participants by email. Information can be shared by keeping files in shared folders. Into runs under the MS-DOS operating system.

- **Right Hand Man (RHM) from Custom:** RHM is a memory resident program that provides more than 17 different facilities via a menu that pops up when the 'hotkey' is depressed. These include an alternative to the telephone - a 'chat' link whereby everything typed at one workstation appears in a window on another screen; a diary, a meeting scheduler, an autodial function (if a modem is connected to the PC) and a card index facility[52].

- **Life from Motorola Computer Systems:** Motorola's Linked Information Environment (LIfe) includes four components called LIfe•Forms - an electronic forms facility; LIfe•Plans - a shared spreadsheet facility; LIfe•Works - a data entry facility; and LIfe•Lines - an email facility. LIfe•Forms enables a forms designer to specify how a new form is to be displayed and printed, and how the input of information is to be contolled. The designer can specify that the nature of the form be altered upon input of specific information.LIfe runs on Motorola computers under the Unix operating system. LIfe•Plans is a fully featured spreadsheet similar to Lotus 1-2-3.

Group Decision Support Systems

- **Aspects from Group Technologies Inc**: This product "allows users to interact in the creation of a document as if they were sitting in front of the same Macintosh screen and taking turns with the mouse. Each of up to 16 users working with a document get their own cursor, enabling many changes to be made simultaneously. Aspects allows various degrees of conference formality, so on-line meetings can range from highly managed briefings to free-for-all brainstorming sessions."[53].

Advanced Meeting Room Systems

- **The POD from ICL**: The POD is a purpose-built environment designed to support groups of managers. In physical terms it is an octagonal meeting room with a central round table, large screens, whiteboards and hand-held controllers. The screens allow projection of 35 mm and OHP slides, video tape, TV broadcasts and outputs from other applications running on the POD's computer system. The POD's modular construction can be configured to suit particular needs, and enable it to be installed in only a few days. The standard twelve-person configuration has external dimensions of a 7 metres square with the main meeting room forming an octagonal area within it.

- **Transview Memory from Davis**: Transparent, flat, liquid crystal display panels placed on an overhead slide projector can display images created on a linked PC. Several flat panel products of this type have become available recently - but the Transview provides greater portability by dispensing with the need for the PC. Instead the Transview has a built in disc drive and generates the images directly from the disc. All functions can be controlled from a hand-held remote-control pad[54].

- **Large Area Display from Greyhawk**: Based on liquid crystal light valve technology, the Large Area Display offers a screen size up to 2x3 metres and can display up to 16 million colours. It displays flicker free continuous tone images at a 5000 x 7500 pixel resolution. A selective erase feature allows image montages to be created and the display to be used interactively.

- **TeamWorker from Decision Dynamics Ltd**: "With TeamWorker, each group member has a personal handset - like a video remote control - comprising a keypad and two-line display. This enables individual options, beliefs, judgements, decisions, feelings and preferences to be input and then transmitted to a receiver. This is linked to a microcomputer so that inputs are recorded, analysed and displayed as needed on a large screen or monitor."[55].

- **GroupSystems from Ventana**: GroupSystems is an integrated set of 20 software modules supporting meeting activities such as electronic brainstorming, idea organisation, voting, alternatives evaluation and policy formation. The system links 8 - 25 MS-DOS personal computers connected by a local area network. Use of the system is controlled from a facilitator's station which also controls what appears on the public wall screen.

Team Development and Management Tools

- **SuperSync from SwixTech:** This package is designed to analyse group behaviour either to support the creation of teams or to provide feedback to teams about their interactivity. To use it, the names of the individuals concerned are listed and the questions they are to answer, selected. Questions can be created or those included in the program can be used (for example, 'You will most probably obtain the best advice from whom?'). The programme prints the questionnaire which the individuals concerned are asked to complete. Upon feeding back the results into SuperSync, bar charts are produced showing centres of influence etc.[50].

- **Syzygy from Information Research Corporation:** Syzygy combines workgroup scheduling with a strong slant towards aspects of project management. It includes a hierarchical Activity List, multi-level project management-style Gantt charts, a calendar and a to-do list. The product is built around the concept that activities stem from objectives and that objectives are accomplished by creating, assigning and completing projects. Projects, in turn, break down into tasks[49]. Notes can be attached to tasks either beforehand to explain what to do, or after the fact to explain what happened. Managers can delegate tasks, complete with schedules and detailed instructions, to subordinates or co-workers, and then monitor progress[17].

- **Netmap from Netmap Limited:** With Netmap, individuals are given simple questionnaires to fill in. The results enable communications between and within formal / functional groups to be identified. The results are displayed graphically in circular network 'maps'. This enables participants to understand how the organisation functions in real terms, who speaks to who about what, how often and how important that communication is[3].

Appendix B   Descriptions of Research Projects

The purpose of this appendix is to give readers a clearer view of the CSCW-related research that is currently being conducted. It is not a comprehensive listing, and inclusion or exclusion from this appendix implies nothing.

B.1 COST Co-Tech Projects

Projects in a 1992-1994 COST Co-Tech Action may include some or all of the following.

IT support for Group Knowledge Development (ITSforGK)

- Whenever a group of people is confronted with a common task they need to establish some common knowledge. The major goals of this project are to investigate the process of group knowledge development and to assess how technology could be made to support it. The project will first review relevant literature in a range of disciplines including philosophy, anthropology, organisational theory, social psychology, and artificial intelligence. A knowledge sharing prototype system is being developed and used by the group to review the literature and to undertake empirical studies. The project will identify requirements for group knowledge development support tools and then match available technology to those requirements. **Contact:** Paul Wilson

CSCW Environment

- Current CSCW applications are often unaware of the existence of other applications and provide few mechanisms for working in conjunction with other applications. The goal of this project is to define a CSCW environment which supports interoperability between a variety of CSCW applications, and which supports the co-existence of remote and local cooperation, personal and group working, and synchronous and asynchronous working. The project will start by analysing example application areas and existing CSCW tools to identify requirements. Then a model will be developed and iteratively evaluated and improved by applying it to other application areas. **Contact:** Wolfgang Prinz

Cooperative Multimedia Processes (COMMPOSITE)

- This project will focus on cooperative activities that will benefit from technological advances in multimedia workstations and high-speed networks. Activities to be considered include shared design and document-handling, monitoring of process control plants, and team tasks such as handling of emergencies. The aim is to investigate the effects on multimedia architectures of different temporal, spatial and organisational constraints. The project will start by reviewing existing research and establishing methodologies for investigating remote cooperation. Experimental work across multiple sites will be used to evaluate and develop appropriate models, architectures and ways of working. **Contact:** Sylvia Wilbur

CSCW Systems Design Concepts (DECO)

- Experience with CSCW systems development indicates a gap between the conceptual foundations of CSCW systems design and the reality encountered by CSCW systems in cooperative work settings. The aim of this project is to systematically evaluate existing CSCW design techniques, and to act as a focus for sponsoring and developing more adequate approaches. Early work in the project will maintain the emphasis on case studies, leading to the development of suggested approaches later. To ensure feedback on the utility of the concepts being developed, members will encourage design teams to work with and develop the concepts. Finally the conceptual and methodological results will be exemplified by developing an outline design for a CSCW system in conjunction with practitioners in a specific application domain.

Contact: Mike Robinson

Interdisciplinary Theory (INTACT)

- A multitude of disciplines contribute to the support of cooperative work (for example, software engineering, networking, systems design, cognitive ergonomics, linguistics, anthropology, social psychology, sociology). The project aims to explore and develop the contributions that each discipline can make, and to establish an interdisciplinary theoretical base for CSCW. The project will start by identifying relevant disciplines and their contribution to CSCW. Examples of applications and empirical studies will be analysed to derive the implicit and explicit assumptions they invoke, and to suggest a task taxonomy of cooperation. A second stage will evaluate complementary and contesting concepts and terminology from which a reference model for cooperation technology will be deduced. The project will produce a preliminary interdisciplinary theory for cooperation technology; an initial set of interdisciplinary application concepts and models; suggested guidelines for methods, tools and good interdisciplinary practice; and a specification for a future interdisciplinary empirical research project.

Contact: Gerrit C. van der Veer

Reference Model for CSCW Systems Support

- The project aims to develop a homogeneous technical framework, or reference model, for describing and realising multimedia CSCW systems. The model will consist of a descriptions of common CSCW functions and services for a platform supporting the development and interworking of CSCW applications; and a generic architecture for such a CSCW platform. The functions and services will be divided in two groups - those that are application-specific and those that are generally useful for a range of CSCW tasks. The reference model will be developed after considering existing relevant architectures and the needs of multimedia applications and other new technologies. The model's suitability will be evaluated in conjunction with other Co-Tech projects.

Contact: Kjell Age Bringsrud

Distributed Meetings

- In recent years the concept of Computer Aided Team meeting rooms to support teams meeting face-to-face at one location, has been extensively developed and tested. However, the trend of internationalisation of organisations and the dispersal of specialists to multiple sites, demands that such electronic meeting rooms are capable of being linked. The aim of this project is to determine the technology required to connect the infrastructures of two or more electronic meeting rooms, and to establish what tools are required to enable teams in different meeting rooms to interwork. The work will be based around the two electronic meeting rooms already in place at the University of Hohenheim and the University of Amsterdam respectively. Interconnection of

the two rooms presents a realistically difficult challenge in that they run on different platforms (DOS and Apple) and they will be connected via two different national telecoms services.
Contact: Helmut Krcmar

Interface Requirements for Multimedia Cooperative Systems (U-CERAMICS)

• This project will investigate the implications for user interface design of the use of multimedia environments for cooperative work. User issues as opposed to technical issues will be addressed; for example, the quality of interaction, stress caused by the system, user satisfaction and impact on quality of working life. These topics will be investigated by doing experimental work from which will emerge a report classifying and describing the potential impact of multimedia communications technology on the working life of users.
Contact: Steve Guest

B.2 ESPRIT Projects

Descriptions of ESPRIT CSCW-related projects are shown below.

MULTIWORKS

• MULTIWORKS - development of a multimedia office workstation.
• Project 2105; started January 1989; ran initially for 24 months.
• Organisations participating in the project include Olivetti, AEG Olympia, Bull, Acorn Computers, SGS-Thomson, TA-Triumph-Adler, Philips, Harlequin and Chorus Systems.

MULTIWORKS is building an office workstation that manipulates video, graphics, text, voice and sound, and that complies with international standards. Two configurations are being developed: a high-cost authoring workstation (MIW), and a low-cost delivery system (MIW-L). MIW is based on an open 32-bit architecture with intelligent controllers to manage multimedia devices. Multiworks will include new interaction devices such as voice input and electronic paper; an enhanced version of Unix to handle multimedia; an object-oriented programming environment for developing traditional applications that use the new media; and a set of authoring tools based on hypertext and expert systems.
Contact: G. Ciardiello

Emergency Management Support (ISEM)

• IT Support for Emergency Management (ISEM).
• Project 2322; started January 1989; runs for 39 months.
• Organisations participating include Risoe National Laboratory, Creon Application Development, Technical Research Centre of Finland, Scaitech, Dansk Internationalt, Tecnatom, Tecnicas Reunidas, Enea, Jydsk Telefon, Uitesa, Studsvik Nuclear, IGC-Inspection Y Garantia de Calidad and GRS.

ISEM aims to develop an integrated information system capable of supporting the complex, dynamic, distributed decision-making associated with the management of emergencies. The project will define a system architecture and develop an application generator to support the system life-cycle. The development will be driven by requirements identified by emergency management organisations in both the nuclear power generation and chemical products industries. The system will be designed to serve as a dedicated support tool for decision makers who manage rare but potentially severe events.
Contact: Verner Andersen

Elusive Office (ELO)

- Elusive Office (ELO).
- Project 2382; started January 1989; runs for 48 months.
- Organisations participating include Empirica, CLS Computer Lernsysteme, Standard Elektrik Lorenz, Rutherford Appleton Laboratory, Fraunhofer Institute, Oeva-Versicherungen and Realace.

The ELO project is addressing the requirements of office workers who routinely work away from company offices. Its objective is to develop a system which provides maximum flexibility in work location and working time, and which allows the mobile worker to communicate from any possible location. The results of the project will be an ELO hardware demonstrator and a highly integrated set of software and tools. The hardware will consist of a modular combination of laptopcomputers, portable fax and portable peripheral input/output devices such as printers and scanners.
Contact: W. Korte

Intelligent Agents for Knowledge Workers (KWICK)

- Knowledge workers intelligently collecting, coordinating and consulting knowledge (KWICK).
- Project 2466; started March 1989; runs for 36 months.
- Organisations participating include Bull, Iriam, Tecograf Software, AIS, Elsevier Science Publishers, ISPRA, Universita Di Milano, University of Glasgow, CMSU;-Communication & Management Systems, Espasa Calpe and CNRS.

KWICK will provide scientific and technical knowledge workers with an environment aimed at improving the productivity and quality of their work. Based on a distributed client-server architecture integrating artificial intelligence and hypermedia technologies, KWICK will provide easy access to knowledge and computational resources, and to support services. The user will be assisted by 'intelligent agents', and will be able to define new agents with the aid of existing agents and by using powerful object-oriented tools.
Contact: A. Cicu

Multiparty Desktop Video conferencing (MIAS)

- Multipoint Interactive Audiovisual System (MIAS).
- Project 2684; started February 1989; ran initailly for 24 months.
- Organisations participating include BT, Alcatel CIT, Cselt-Centro Studi e Laboratori Telecomunicazioni, PTT Research Neher Labs, Telefonica Investigacion Y Desarrollo, CNET and Amper.

MIAS is developing a signal and protocol infrastructure to support multipoint desktop video conferencing and multimedia interactions via ISDN and higher bit-rate systems. The project's final demonstrator will be a multimedia system with visual and office system aids and able to interwork between different terminal types. Transmission costs will be reduced by choosing the minimum bit-rate needed for each particular facility.
Contact: W. Clark

Distributed Cooperative Work (EUROCOOP)

- IT Support for Distributed Cooperative Work (EUROCOOP).
- Project 5303; started January 1991; runs for 36 months.
- Organisations participating include TA-Triumph-Adler, Empirica, Jydsk Telefon, BNR Europe, X-Tel Services, Aarhus University, Rutherford Appleton Laboratory, Great Belt and GMD.

EUROCOOP aims to develop systems to support distributed cooperative work such as the formation of joint ventures and the planning and carrying out of large-scale technical projects. Support will be provided for joint authoring and editing of documents, the scheduling and coordination of collaborative activities, progress monitoring, formal reporting and exception management. Detailed studies of requirements will focus on the needs of those organisations currently involved in constructing a combined bridge and tunnel over the Great Belt in Denmark.
Contact: Klaus Kreplin

Models of Cooperative Work (PECOS)

- Perspectives on Cooperative Systems (PECOS).
- Project 5660; started January 1991; runs for 12 months.
- Organisations participating include AIS-Artificial Intelligence Software, Bikit-Babbage Institute for Knowledge & IT, Industrias de Telecomunication, Mari Computer Systems, Lombardia Informatica, Emmepi and Universidad Politecnica de Madrid.

This is an Esprit exploratory action which will investigate models for CSCW. The study will focus on the concept of intelligent agents (which may be either human users or intelligent software modules) and schemes of cooperation which enable such agents to collaborate successfully in achieving goals. Project outputs will include a report and two small animation prototypes.
Contact: Richard Power

Multi-Agent Environment (IMAGINE)

- Integrated Multi-Agent Interactive Environment (IMAGINE).
- Project 5362; started January 1991; runs for 60 months.
- Organisations participating include Siemens, Intrasoft, Steria, Imperial College of Science Technology & Medecine, Rijks Universiteit Leiden, University of Keele, Plessey Research.

The IMAGINE project aims to provide a sophisticated and comprehensive environment upon which a variety of multi-agent systems can be built. It will be able to support systems requiring a high level of cooperation among heterogenous autonomous agents, including humans, in order to produce qualitatively better results than could otherwise be achieved. A multi-agent language will be developed with which to specify agent models, cooperation models, information exchange, controls, operations or protocols for multi-agent systems. The language will be prototyped using Parlog and Prolog and subsequently implemented in C++.
Contact: Hans Haugeneder

B.3 UK Advanced Technology Programme Projects

Details of CSCW-related projects in the ATP programme are shown below.

Requirements for Remote Cooperation

- Establishing the communicational requirements of IT systems that support humans cooperating remotely (ROCOCO).
- Project 1225 - £190,000 started August 1989, runs for 3 years.
- Being undertaken by the LUTCHI Research Centre at Loughborough University ('uncled' by TDS Ltd.).
Contact: Steve Scrivener

Cooperation of Dispersed Teams

- Aide-de-Camp (facilitating the cooperative working of dispersed teams).
- Project 2119 - £98,000 started February 1991, runs for 3 years.
- Being undertaken by Liverpool University ('uncled' by the Electricity Council Research Centre).
  Contact: Michael Shave

Cooperative Requirements Capture

- Cooperative requirements capture
- Project 1130 - £433,000 started March 1990, runs for 3 years.
- Being undertaken by ICL, Brameur, Human Technology and the University of Manchester Institute of Science & Technology.
  Contact: Linda Macaulay

Multimedia User Modelling

- Multimedia user modelling systems.
- Project 1256 - £997,000 started September 1989, runs for 3 years.
- Being undertaken by Loughborough University and Queen Mary & Westfield College.
  Contact: Peter Johnson

B.4 Projects in the UK Joint Council Initiative

Descriptions of CSCW-related projects funded by the Joint Council initiative in Cognitive Science and Human-Computer Interaction, are shown below (these descriptions have been kindly provided by the Joint Council initiative).

Emergence of social complexity

- A Distributed Artificial Intelligence Based Investigation into the Emergence of Social Complexity.
- Project 8930879 starting Oct 1990, running for 36 months.
- Being undertaken by Computer Science Dept & Cognitive Science Centre, University of Essex; Department of Sociology, University of Surrey; Department of Archaeology, University of Cambridge.

The purpose of the project is:
(1) to use the concepts and techniques of distributed artificial intelligence (DAI) to give a precise computational interpretation to the process model for the emergence of social complexity proposed by Mellars, and to demonstrate its basic coherence at the DAI level;
(2) to study in detail the properties of the central feedback loop of the model and its side effects; and
(3) to relate experimental conclusions to the understanding of the processes by which social complexity emerged in the Upper Palaeolithic, and to the archaeology thereof.
Contacts: J.Doran, G.Gilbert and P.Mellars (only Mr Gilbert's address is provided in Appendix D).

The Problem of Joint Action

- A multidisciplinary exploration of the problem of joint action.
- Project 8917838 starting January 1990, running for 36 months.
- Being undertaken by the Department of Psychology, Nottingham University.

The purpose of the project is:
(1) to integrate information on the nature of jointly conceived and executed actions, from different disciplines within (and adjoining) Cognitive Science, so as to bring ideas and advances that any of them suggest, to bear on issues which they all find problematic;

(2) to extend the range of the cognitive sciences beyond the actions of individuals, which they have always considered, to the problems of joint action, which they have tackled less often with less success; (3) to lay the conceptual groundwork for a kind of IT which would act in collaboration with people, rather than responding to or issuing their instructions to act, sharing the initiative, and perhaps even the responsibility for jointly made plans, policies, decisions and actions; (4) to provide guidelines and suggest methodologies for modellers and programmers, created by the panel of experts assembled for this project. These would act as design heuristics, presented with their advantages and disadvantages and would concern such things as sub-goal/end-goal relations; the management of error, uncertainty, ambiguity and risk; the use of fall-back strategies and contingency plans; and the choice between collaborative and competitive principles for outcome selection. Also guidance on psychological issues associated with joint action, such as trust, allegiance and coalition, group formation and differentiation, and the tension between individual and collective rationality will be produced.
Contacts: David Clarke.

Collaborative Writing

- The development of a cognitive model for computer support of collaborative writing.
- Project 8919574 starting October 1990, running for 24 months.
- Being undertaken by the School of Cognitive and Computing Sciences, University of Sussex.

The purpose of the project is:
(1) to develop an integrated model of the social processes of collaboration and the cognitive processes involved in writing. The model will be both reactive, describing current practices in collaborative writing, and proactive, informing the design of new multi-author writing support systems through the identification of new practical methods of collaboration and a metalanguage and conversational structure to assist communication between writers;
(2) to implement, test and refine the model through its embodiment as a tool for the support of collaborative writing.
Contact: Michael Sharples.

Social Knowledge Representation

- Social Knowledge Representation: an anthropological perspective.
- Project 8920754 starting January 1990, running for 36 months.
- Being undertaken by Computing Dept, Imperial College, London.

The purpose of the project is:
(1) to model complex multi-agent systems with a particular focus on "exteriorised" knowledge structures such as culture, ritual and institution, and related structures such as socialisation;
(2) to formally model the properties of exteriorised knowledge structures which are maintained by, and maintain, multi-agent systems. Specifically to determine:
- how knowledge taken from external sources, a tradition, culture, authority or media - knowledge whose derivation and validation is unknown or unavailable - influences agents;
- how agents use and articulate such knowledge, particularly its distribution, interpretation and modification as the environment and multi-agent system changes;

- the degree to which multi-agent systems preserve variant interpretations and different views of knowledge within, and between, agents;
- the variability in the interpretation of common or shared experience, and the way such variability contributes to the robustness and adaptability of a system confronted with changing circumstances.

Contact: Anthony Finkelstein and Michael Fischer (only Anthony Finkelstein's address is provided in Appendix D).

Modelling Organisational Knowledge

- Interactive generative organisational frame of reference.
- Project 8920539 starting January 1990, running for 30 months.
- Being undertaken by Dept. of Social Psychology, London School of Economics.

The purpose of the project is:
(1) to create an interactive and generative version of the Generic Organisational Frame of Reference (GOFOR) which offers modelling organisational knowledge and understanding of organisational reality from a systems point of view;
(2) to design and develop an interactive computer based version of GOFOR (IGOFOR) which will be enhanced and validated through real-life field tests secured through its adoption by teams of analysts employed in a wide range of cases at departments, institutional, national and international agency level, studied in international projects and consultancies in which LSE is participating;
(3) to provide an efficient introduction route to researchers and professionals in the field, so that IGFOR may find applications guiding the organisational investigations and modelling processes and helping in the recognition of problems relevant to the implementation of organisational changes and their effects.
Contact: Patrick Humphreys.

B.5 NSF Projects

Descriptions of projects funded by the US National Science Foundation programme in Coordination Theory and Collaboration Technology, are shown below (these descriptions have been kindly provided by NSF).

Support for the Electronic Artifacts of Scientific Culture

- Academic Institutional Memory: Analyzing the Electronic Artifacts of Scientific Culture.
- $70,000 starting in 1989, running for 12 months
- Being undertaken by the Department of Computer Science & Engineering and by the Department of Cognitive Science, University of California - San Diego.

The goals of the project are to refine a set of tools that encourage researchers to increase their use of electronic information sources during research; to incorporate machine learning mechanisms that are capable of transforming these researchers' browsing behaviors into self-organising information structures; and then to analyse the information structures built manually by the researchers and automatically by the learning mechanisms, as artifacts created by the cultural process of science.
Contacts: Richard Belew & Edwin Hutchins (only Richard Belew's address is provided in Appendix D).

Coordination in Distributed Organisations

- A Normative-Descriptive Theory of Coordination in Distributed Organizations.
- $963,162 starting in 1989, running for 36 months.
- Being undertaken by the Departments of Psychology, Computer Science and Engineering Electrical and Systems Engineering, The University of Connecticut; in collaboration with the Department of Electrical Engineering & Computer Science, MIT, the Fuqua School of Business, Duke University and Alphatech, Inc.

The goal of this project is to quantify the coordination strategies within a human team that are prevalent in their information-processing, situation assessment, resource allocation and task sequencing activities. The researchers are using experimental methods and analytic research to learn: How should and do teams coordinate information, resources, and tasks in an organisation? How should and do teams adapt their coordination strategies in the face of increased uncertainty, time pressure and/or workload? How should databases be organised to efficiently support and enhance human coordination in distributed information processing, resource allocation and task sequencing team situations.
Contacts: David Kleinman, Peter Luh, Krishna Pattipati, Fred Maryanski, Robert Shaw (only David Kleinman's address is provided in Appendix D).

Representing and Supporting Coordination

- Representing and Supporting Coordination.
- $298,500 starting in 1989, running for 36 months.
- Being undertaken by Sloan School of Management, MIT.

This project aims to build a general tool for supporting cooperative work and personal information management. The researchers are experimenting with applications that help people:
(a) find intelligently, sort, and prioritize electronic messages;
(b) monitor task responsibilities and deadlines in large projects
(c) manage complex design changes in engineering groups;
(d) analyse the various arguments and counter arguments for decisions they must make; and
(e) write documents to which many people contribute.
These applications will be combined in a consistent framework to let ordinary people create and modify them for themselves. The work will build on an existing prototype system that lets people define and manipulate "semi-structured objects" to represent things such as people, tasks, products, messages and companies. Users represent elationships between these objects (such as between people and their supervisors) by "hypertext links," and summarise data about groups of objects in tables or graphs. Users can create "intelligent agents" that use sets of rules to automatically process information.
Contacts: Thomas Malone & John Carroll (only Thomas Malone's address is provided in Appendix D).

Relating Market Concepts to Coordination

- Coordinating Multi-Processor Organizations.
- $634,202 starting in 1989, running for 24 months.
- Being undertaken by the Electronic Research Laboratory and the Depts of Economics Electrical Engineering and Computer Science, Industrial Engineering and Operations Research, the University of California - Berkeley.

This interdisciplinary effort is motivated by parallel problems in computer science and economics. Economists have long been intrigued with the idea that a market can be viewed as a device for dividing up a gigantic computational task (finding an efficient allocation of resources) among many simultaneously functioning persons and processors. If that device is indeed the "cheapest" way of performing the overall task (as economists traditionally claim), then that fact ought to have interesting implications for the design of cheap distributed computing schemes in general. On the other hand, general results about cheap distributed computing, based on models of real computing and communication technologies, ought to provide fresh and more convincing ways to support or to refute the economists' traditional claim. The research will investigate six related problems in each of which there is a group of processors/ persons who are to perform a common task. A designer will choose a coordination scheme that specifies for each person/ processor the computations and communicating to be performed at each of a sequence of points in time. The designer wants the scheme to be efficient with respect to several cost measures such as communication time, computing capacity, distance from correct task fulfillment, and the capacity to control actions. The researchers will also devote considerable effort to developing a precise common language for exploring problems of coordination.

Contacts: Thomas Marschak, Pravin Varaiya, Eugene Lawler, Shmuel Oren & Umesh Vazirani (only Thomas Marschak's address is provided in Appendix D).

Support for Co-Authoring

- The "Work in Preparation"(PREP) Editor: Support for Co-Authoring and Commenting.
- $950,000 starting in 1989, running for 36 months.
- Being undertaken by the Department of Computer Science, the Department of English and the Information Technology Center, Carnegie Mellon University.

The goal of this project is to develop the PREP editor to study co-authoring and commenting relationships across local and remote networks. In developing this editor, the researchers will pay special attention to three aspects of collaboration: support for social interaction among co-authors; support for cognitive aspects of co-authoring and external commenting; and, support for practicality in both types of interaction. The project will contribute to the further refinement and test of a collaborative model of how groups usefully interact when working together as co-authors and commenters. It will also provide a proof of concept test for editing systems that support structured collaboration among authors as well as the efficient management of large volumes of comments that external commenters can make on authors' working drafts. The editor's architecture will be sensitive to the desirability for studying copyright issues. The researchers see this problem as one closely related to that of giving timely feedback to readers (in this case, to the readers of the text and to the owners of the copyright).

Contacts: James Morris, David Kaufer, Christine Neuwrith and Ravinder Chandok (only James Morris' address is provided in Appendix D).

Collaboration Technology for Software Design Teams

- Technology Support for Collaborative Workgroups.
- $825,000 starting in 1989, running for 36 months.
- Being undertaken by the Depts of Psychology, Electrical Engineering & Computer Science, Computer & Information Systems, and the Cognitive Science & Machine Intelligence Laboratory at the University of Michigan; in collaboration with Bill Curtis, Simon Gibbs and Gail Rein of the Microelectronics & Computer Technology Corporation; and with William Sasso of the Center for Strategic Technology Research of Arthur Andersen.

This project will examine how a small group of collaborators work together to design software requirements, and what impact the use of groupware has. The research will study both current practice and groupware-supported collaboration. Existing observational and interview data will be examined to identify opportunities for technology support. In addition new observational studies of software design teams will be conducted, primarily at Arthur Andersen, to identify opportunities for technology experiments and to establish a baseline of present practice. During the project several experimental groupware systems will be built and evaluated. **Contacts:** Gary Olson, Elliot Soloway, Judith Olson, Steven Lytinen, Daniel Atkins & Lynn Conway (only Gary Olson's address is provided in Appendix D).

Decision Making in the Corporate Planning Process

- Coordination of Distributed Decision Making in a Corporate Planning Environment.
- $210,000 starting in 1990, running for 24 months.
- Being undertaken by Case Western Reserve University.

In distributed decision environments, intelligent agents at network nodes interact with private databases, common databases, and each other to coordinate their independent actions. This project explores how human, organisational, and technological elements in a distributed corporate planning setting, condition the level of coordination and integration of the agents' individual plans. The researchers will work with the Management Systems Research Group of Digital Equipment Corporation (DEC); to develop, test and evaluate decision support facilities for their individual, autonomous planning decisions. The researchers will evaluate the outcomes of system use among a set of interdependent business unit managers in terms of the coordination and integration of their individual plans as a whole, as well as the level of trust, commitment, understanding and cooperation they experience in this distributed planning setting. **Contact:** Richard J. Boland.

Coordination in Software Engineering

- Flexible Coordination in Collaborative Software Engineering.
- $160,000 starting in 1990, running for 24 months.
- Being undertaken by Purdue University.

Traditional support for coordinating the activities of collaborative software engineers consists mainly of version control and mail systems and does not meet the requirements of many software engineering tasks such as interactive group design and debugging. This project will investigate flexible coordination of the activities of cooperating software engineers. In particular, an approach will be developed allowing a range of concurrency control mechanisms;

alerters automatically informing users of events in which they are interested; dynamic variable-grained locking; and live sound integrated with the concurrency control mechanism. The researchers will also study how a particular scheme can be automatically chosen by the system based on a minimum performance level requested by the user. Prototype demonstrator applications will be developed.
Contact: Presun Dewan.

Coordination Protocols for Intelligent Agents

- A Hierarchical Negotiation Protocol Using Multi-Dimensional Behavior Specifications.
- $165,000 starting in 1990, running for 24 months.
- Being undertaken by the University of Michigan.

This research is directed towards integrating concepts from artificial intelligence, organisation theory, and operations research into a single framework. The research argument is that the plans, organisations, and schedules studied in these separate fields can share a common representation, and are simply different abstractions of a behavioral specification. The research outlines a protocol for coordination whereby intelligent agents incrementally exchange behavioral information and search through alternative behaviors to resolve conflicts and promote cooperation. The research also implements and evaluates this framework both in the context of a cooperative robotics domain, and in the context of an intelligent system for scheduling meetings between people.
Contact: Edmund Durfee.

Support for Collaborative Design Teams

- Supporting Collaborative Design with Integrated Knowledge-Based Design Environments.
- $700,000 starting in 1990, running for 36 months.
- Being undertaken by the University of Colorado.

The goal of this project is to develop a conceptual framework and a prototype system for collaboration in an asynchronous mode among members of design teams. The proposed design environments include knowledge-based and graphic construction components with issue-based hypermedia systems designed to support collaboration. The application domain for the prototype system is the design of communications networks within buildings. The complexity of such projects forces large and heterogeneous groups to work together over long periods of time. The large and growing discrepancy between the amount of potentially relevant knowledge for the design task and the amount any one designer can know and remember puts limits on progress in design. Overcoming this limit is a central challenge for developers of systems that support both individual and collaborative design efforts.
Contacts: Gerhard Fischer, Andreas Lemke, Raymond McCall (only Gerhard Fischer's address is provided in Appendix D).

Practical Constraints on Decision Making

- Decision-Making Based on Practical Knowledge.
- $300,000 starting in 1990, running for 24 months.
- Being undertaken by Yale University.

How to make decisions in the face of uncertainty is a core problem in many computer science and economic modelling problems. However, there are a number of weaknesses in the traditional

approaches to modelling knowledge, including the assumptions that there are perfect reasoners and that inferences can be based on arbitrarily deep levels of knowledge. This project aims to develop a new notion of practical knowledge upon which to base coordinated decision making. Practical knowledge will take account of several factors which limit a reasoner's deductive ability such as computational resources available to the reasoner, imperfections in the reasoner's ability to carry out correct deductions, and faultiness and incompleteness in the data available to the reasoner. Many of these factors have been studied previously in isolation. This research will extend and unify such work to establish a comprehensive theory of sound reasoning in a practical multi-agent environment.
Contacts: Michael Fischer, John Geanakoplos, Lenore Zuck (only Michael Fischer's address is provided in Appendix D).

Distributed Group Decision Making

- Distributed Group Support Systems.
- $184,883 starting in 1990, running for 36 months.
- Being undertaken by New Jersey Institute of Technology.

The primary objective of the project is to build a general theory, supported by empirical evidence, to understand how variations in group structures and software tools affect the process and outcome of decision making. This multi-disciplinary effort focusses on synchronous computer conferences in which participants are distributed in different locations, and on asynchronous computer conferences in which participation is distributed in time and space.
Contact: Starr Roxanne Hiltz.

Coordination in Contemporary Information Systems

- Real Time, Interactive Information Systems.
- $450,000 starting in 1990, running for 36 months.
- Being undertaken by the University of California at Irvine.

This study investigates aspects of the role of computerized information systems as instruments of coordination in complex organisations. Questions addressed include: What kinds of coordination problems do computerized systems actually resolve, and to what extent? And what social and economic impacts result from the use of such systems? The research will gather empirical data through cross sectional studies, comparative case studies and a longitudinal survey of manufacturing firms with relatively structured systems characterisable as Computer Integrated Manufacturing.
Contacts: Rob Kling, Kenneth Kraemer, Vijay Gurbaxani, Yannis Bakos, John King (only Rob Kling's address is in Appendix D).

Interfaces for Collaborative Work

- Fractal Interfaces for Collaborative Work.
- $160,000 starting in 1990, running for 24 months.
- Being undertaken by New York University.

The object of this research effort is to exploit a wholly new interactive window concept, already experimentally implemented in the laboratory, as a basis for construction of flexible new forms of collaboration environments. These environments will allow collaborators to work within a shared information space whose structure adjusts easily and whose visual form naturally expresses the inherent structure of their collaboration. The first stage of this research is to define and implement a basic collection of functions in

an interactive zoomable window system. This system will then be extended across a network, thereby making available a shared information space which will allow an arbitrary number of users to work in a common virtual environment, each possibly enjoying a different view of this environment.
Contact: Kenneth Perlin.

Systems Technology for a Collaboratory

- Systems Technology for Building a National Collaboratory.
- $1,130,000 starting in 1990, running for 36 months.
- Being undertaken by University of Arizona.

This project is to develop the systems technology necessary to build a nationwide information infrastructure for the scientific community, and to demonstrate this technology by applying it to a mini-collaboratory for a specific community of molecular biologists that studies the genetic structure of the C. Elegans nematode. The goals are to collect the community knowledge into a digital library, develop the technology to manipulate the library, and to learn how to facilitate effective utilization of this technology for sizeable communities. This mini-collaboratory will take advantage of the underlying communication support provided by NSFNET to support users nationwide. Key problems to be addressed include designing bulk transfer protocols that facilitate the rapid movement of data across wide area networks; discovering efficient data clustering and caching strategies; providing a uniform interface for displaying, editing, searching and grouping a wide range of complex objects; and supporting directory services that can be used to located many distributed resources.
Contacts: Bruce Schatz, Larry Peterson, Scott Hudson (only Bruce Schatz's address is provided in Appendix D).

Group Collaboration in a Collaboratory

- Building and Using a Collaboratory: A Foundation for Supporting and Studying Group Collaborations.
- $900,000 starting in 1990, running for 36 months.
- Being undertaken by University of North Carolina at Chapel Hill.

This project focuses on experimental observation of groups doing real collaborative work and using systems and communications media explicitly designed to aid their tasks. The results will expand understanding of how people collaborate and of how to design systems that augment collaborative activities. The project has five interdependent components:
(1) a theoretical foundation for observing and understanding the social and cognitive aspects of group collaborations;
(2) tools for rapid prototyping and reconfiguration of application environments for use by working groups, and multi-media communications to support multi-person interactions;
(3) protocol analysis tools to record and study how individuals and groups interact through the networked computer environment;
(4) application testbed systems (generic and domain specific) that can be used by groups engaged in real work; and
(5) group studies and experiments to test system, social and cognitive hypotheses.
Contacts: John Smith, Donelson Smith, Peter Calingaert, Kevin Jeffay, Dorothy Holland, John Hayes (only John Smith's address is provided in Appendix D).

Collaboration Using Hypertext

- Distributed Concurrent Hypertext for Multi-reader Cooperative Systems.
- $90,000 starting in 1990, running for 24 months.
- Being undertaken by the Computer & Information Sciences department, University of Florida (Gainesville) and the department of Computer Science, University of Maryland.

This project aims to develop a system allowing rapid prototyping and evaluation of collaboration support structures. It will operate in the context of a data browsing and information system based on the Trellis model of hypertext. Trellis uses a formally defined concurrent process model (Petri nets) to implement hypertext. Trellis documents have a well defined and analysable formal structure, and the concurrency aspects of Petri nets enable Trellis to manage groups of interactive agents within the structure of a linked document. Trellis documents not only represent relations among information elements, but also serve as the basis for construction of high-level cooperative process descriptions in which the agents of computation are coarse grained and of moderate speed and number. This corresponds to groups of people interacting cooperatively on the solution of a problem involving the browsing and manipulation of information.
Contacts: David Stotts.

B.6 UK CSCW Research

Some of the organisations undertaking CSCW research in the UK are listed below. Note that inclusion of an organisation in the list does not necessarily mean that all the CSCW work being undertaken within its confines is included.

BICC Technologies

The BICC's Systems Development Centre (SDC) supports BICC Technologies - a systems and electronics group whose main activities lie in communications, controls, information technology and integrated building management systems. The SDC has been investigating multimedia systems since 1987. Its most recent interest has been to build a prototype system as part of RACE project 1039 (DIMUN - Distributed International Manufacturing Using Networks). The current system, known as MILAN (Multimedia Industrial LAN) concentrates on the integration of voice, video and data networking techniques to support typical manufacturing tasks carried out by groups of people at a distance.

The system includes software to control various hardware such as telephone, video views, video switching, recording, etc. The software is based on the metaphor of a 'room' in which people can meet to share tools such as the whiteboard (a general sketchpad), and hardware peripherals such as videodiscs, simultaneously. The system is fully distributed with no central machine. It is aimed at supporting informal 'horizontal' communications which are often neglected by formal lines of communication when an organisation is distributed.

The current system is implemented on Apple Macintosh machines, networked over Ethernet. Video is generally analogue using cable TV technology, although long distance digital links over 2Mb/s and 140Mb/s have also been used. Voice can be carried by the video link or over standard PABX facilities under Macintosh control. The main

DIMUN project ended in 1990, but the MILAN part was extended to allow for further demonstrations, including CEBIT '91, and operational trials of CSCW systems within parts of the BICC group. **Contact:** Chris Condon.

BNR Europe Limited

A major focus of work at BNR Europe is the Professional Community Support(PCS) programme, the aim of which is to develop computing infrastructures to permit distributed communities of professionals to work effectively togther. This work is being done as part of BNR Europe's wider concern of pioneering Open Distributed Processing (ODP) technology, through, for example the ESPRIT ISA(ANSA) project.

A number of projects directly support the PCS programme. These include MULTIWORKS, an ESPRIT-II project which is developing the hardware and software for a family of multi-media integrated workstations. MULTIWORKS will provide a workstation-based distributed environment of hyper-media objects, with facilities for shared-window cooperative working developed by the EuroCoOp project. EuroCoOp is an ESPRIT-II project aimed at providing IT (software) support for distributed cooperative work. BNR's system development work under EuroCoOp is particularly concerned to find ODP software architectures which successfully integrate globally-managed group interactions mediated by the execution of pre-allocated process models, with locally managed group interactions supported by shared window/audio/video technologies. **Contact:** Philip Hughes.

Brunel University

Brunel's Department of Computer Science is expanding its existing research base in Knowledge Engineering and Information Systems Design to incorporate CSCW concerns, both theoretical and methodological. The aim is to extend our understanding of the social context of computer use through integration of the methods, perspectives, and findings from Human Sciences in the design of Human-Computer Interfaces; with the social-organisational structure and processes which shape the design and use of knowledge-based and other information systems. This aim is also realized in applications-based research in the domains of business, engineering design and bio-medical research. **Contacts:** Leslie Johnson, Barbara Hulme, Janet McDonnell, Vijay Mittal, Duska Rosenberg, Anthoulis Stylianou, Peter Thomas (only Duska Rosenberg's address is provided in Appendix D).

CSC Europe

CSC Europe's main interest in CSCW is to identify appropriate technologies and techniques which will enable its clients to maintain and develop their positions in rapidly changing world markets. CSC Europe took part in the Cosmos (structured messaging) project and continues to research advanced communication systems (such as desktop video conferencing), group knowledge development, group work design methods and approaches to organisation design and organisational change. A particular interest is to understand the support required by networked organisations (networked in the people sense) distributed across multiple sites and countries. CSC Europe also conducts evaluations of CSCW products, and maintains an overview of current CSCW research worldwide. **Contact:** Paul Wilson.

Hewlett-Packard Laboratories

Hewlett-Packard Laboratories in Bristol has been researching the use and effectiveness of multimedia communication, focusing particularly on desktop video conferencing. Prototype systems running on industry standard PCs using HP's integrated office system NewWave have been been built and are being evaluated. In order to provide for audio and video connections the PC has been modified so that the bezel of the monitor housing contains a miniature camera and a card has been added to display video within a window. No other modifications have been made to the machine. A Unix workstation provides the PCs with network facilities and access to shared resources.

The system provides for the creation and management of voice and video conferences. A directory facility with auto-dialling enables users to make connections easily. Video conferencing over long distances is available to users from their desks using the Integrated Services Digital Network (ISDN) now available from BT.

The system provides a persistent context for audio and video conferences, sharable amongst its users. Users may access documents relevant to the meeting such as agendas, minutes, issue lists, etc. Where the meeting is extended over time or regular, e.g. for weekly sales review meetings, the context will be maintained between meetings. The system also provides users with a shared computer whiteboard on which users can draw or look at a picture of what they are discussing. The image on the whiteboard can also be acquired by cut and paste from other applications.A considerable amount of evaluation work is being done to assess the usefulness of such systems and their applicability to the business environment. **Contact:** Stephen Gale.

Loughborough University of Technology

Loughborough's Department of Computer Studies started a project on "Establishing the communicational requirements of IT systems that support humans cooperating remotely" in collaboration with TDS Ltd. in 1989. The project is due to run until July 1992. The objectives of the project are to investigate communication among persons engaged in computer supported cooperative work, with a view to determining the communication requirements of multi-medium CSCW systems. The research involves establishing the relative usage of the types of communication channel (verbal, pictorial, etc.) routinely involved in proximal cooperative work; investigating the importance of persistent media in CSCW; and exploring the influence of various transient communication media (e.g. speech, gesture) upon successful remote CSCW. The task domain being investigated is the graphic design process. **Contact:** Steve Scrivener.

Queen Mary & Westfield College (QMW), University of London

QMW's department of Computer Science has been involved in CSCW research since acting as the lead partner in the COSMOS project in 1986. In 1990/91 several new projects started, including the TMPI project (funded by BT Research Laboratories), the CoTech project, and the MUMS project. In addition, postgraduate research is being carried out on multimedia Distance Education.

The main focus of the research is on collaboration as a communicative process. COSMOS supported structured asynchronous group communication, in which activities were described in terms of message-passing. In TMPI, initial work concentrated on developing a theoretical approach to synchronous, mixed-media group interaction. A prototype multi-user application has been developed on Macintosh workstations, and patterns of interaction with this system have been analysed. In the second stage of the project, a second application is being developed on a distributed CSCW infrastructure, and a case-study of real-group collaboration will be undertaken.

A second stream of activity in the department is starting in 1991, and will be based on a series of computer teleconferencing experiments to be conducted between QMW and other UK and European sites. These experiments will involve the use of audio and video-conferencing facilities, as well as data communication.

A third project has recently started on Multimedia User Modelling Systems (MUMS), involving QMW and Lutchi, Loughborough. The project is to develop user interaction models considering both multimedia and hypermedia aspects of the interface. The domain for task analysis is to be group decision support for architectural/construction planning.
Contact: Sylvia Wilbur.

Rank Xerox EuroPARC

EuroPARC is currently exploring the possibility of supporting a number of work arrangements and settings by means of various technologies. An integrated multimedia and computational environment has been built to provide the infrastructure for research on interactivity and connectivity in different media. The aim is to understand both the technological possibilities and the social, psychological and organisational dimensions of technological innovations of this kind. The design process has been chosen as the primary research domain for the work. Alongside this experimental work, field studies are being undertaken in a number of different organisations, and attempts are being made to develop collaborative projects with other research groups and organisations.
Contact: Bob Anderson.

University of Manchester Institute of Science & Technology (UMIST)

UMIST's Department of Computation is taking part in the Cooperative Requirements Capture (CRC) project - a collaborative project between UMIST, ICL, Brameur and Human Technology. The aim is to develop prototype tools which can be used to support a multi-disciplinary team in the process of capturing, analysing and documenting the requirements for new computer systems. The underlying method of requirements capture and analysis will be based on the user-centred method USTM (developed under the UK Alvey programme) and is based on face-to-face meetings. The provision of computer support is intended to supplement the face-to-face meetings with the ability for the team to continue their work when geographically dispersed. Investigations are currently underway into the applicability of distributed AI techniques to the design of the associated software support.
Contact: Linda Macaulay.

University of Lancaster

CSCW research at Lancaster takes place within a multi-disciplinary research centre which has members drawn from a number of departments including Psychology, Computer Science and Sociology. The computing department started CSCW work in 1988 during the Alvey ISM project (concerning next-generation Integrated Project Support Environments - IPSEs). Support for clerical information management activities in the software process was investigated, and the work evolved into the development of a structured message system supporting asynchronous cooperative working.

Since then, Lancaster has undertaken other CSCW-related projects, including: Support for Network Management as a Cooperative Activity; Automation of Air Traffic Control (ethnographic studies of air traffic control, in conjunction with the Sociology Department); Support for Cooperative Systems Design; and database requirements for CSCW (this project started in 1991 and runs for two years).

Lancaster's Sociology Department began CSCW work in 1985, taking the automation of air traffic control as an example. Since then it has undertaken CSCW-related research projects on the use of information technology in air traffic control and in the police.

A premise in this research has been that the design of computer support systems typically fails to take account of the social organisation of work. Hence systems may fail because they do not recognise the real nature of tasks, of their working contexts, of the diverse purposes for which they are desired, nor of the requirements they need to fulfil to be usable. The research has used a number of perspectives including the sociology of knowledge, the sociology of organisations, the sociology of the professions, the political economy of technological development, the detailed ethnography of working practices, and a striking expansion into a new field of an ethnomethodological approach.
Contact: Tom Rodden.

University of Manchester

The Psychology department's first involvement with CSCW was with its development of a structure definition language for the Cosmos advanced message system project. This work has evolved into the development of a design methodology for CSCW. The methodology attempts to extend participatory design approaches by incorporating systematic field research techniques (such as ethnography) alongside the modelling of working practices. This has entailed some fundamental work on the nature and significance of formalisms in CSCW, their relation to design and to the accounts of working practices which participants themselves have.

The methodology is intended to respect workers' pre-existing skills and knowledge of their working practices, and to systematically explore junctures within those practices where computer support might be desired by and be useful for workers. The methodology is currently conceived in terms of an ongoing dialogue between an analyst/researcher on the one hand and participants/workers/users on the other. However, it is also intended to foster a vision in which distinctions between the design of work and the work of design might ultimately be dissolved such that design becomes a routine part of work itself. Some aspects of this work have been supported by the UK Government's centre for information systems, CCTA, and it is hoped to undertake trials of the methodology with the collaboration of central government workers.

Several other projects are also underway in connection with social psychological aspects of computer mediated communication and teleworking.
Contact: John Bowers.

University of Nottingham

The Communications Research Group, in the Department of Computer Science, has been involved with the COSMOS, AMIGO, and MacAll projects. Current work includes the two year GRACE project (GRoup ACtivity Environment) which aims to specify and prototype an OSI-based Group Communication Service providing common support services for a wide range of applications.

Members of Nottingham's Psychology Department are interested in work such as the design and evaluation of multimedia tools to support synchronous distributed problem solving; how people construct mental models of complex computer artifacts; and the software development process in large design teams.
Contacts: Peter Bibby, David Gilmore, Claire O'Malley, Hugh Smith (only Claire O'Malley's and Hugh Smith's addresses are provided in Appendix D).

University of Sussex

In October 1990 the School of Cognitive and Computing Sciences started a two year project to investigate Computer Supported Collaborative Writing. The project aims to develop an integrated model of the social processes of collaboration and the cognitive processes involved in writing. The model will be both reactive, describing current practices in collaborative writing, and proactive, informing the design of new multi-author writing support systems, through the identification of new methods of collaboration, and a metalanguage and conversational structure to assist communciation between writers. The project draws upon a number of disciplines, particularly social and cognitive psychology, human-computer interaction, artificial intelligence and linguistics. A thriving research group has developed in association with this project, with interests that include the sociology of small group interaction, computer-supported negotiation, and the external representations used in collaborative writing.
Contact: Mike Sharples.

B.7 Non-UK European CSCW Research

Some of the organisations undertaking CSCW research in non-UK European countries, are listed below. Note that inclusion of an organisation in the list does not necessarily mean that all the CSCW work being undertaken within its confines is included.

Delft University of Technology

In the Psychology Department research is directed at topics in the fields of new information technologies in organisations, and Human Computer Interaction. CSCW-related projects include the following:

(1) User requirements for multimedia applications. This is part of an interdisciplinairy project directed at the development of a

videophone-like application. The research focusses on the relation between the use of different media-channels (face-to-face, text, graphics, sound, video) and taskperformance in a collaborative task in which a taxonomy of cooperative tasks is being developed.

(2) Evaluation studies of (asynchronous) 'Computer Supported Communication' systems in work organisations. The purpose of these studies is to analyse determinants of systems usage, and to discover the implications for communication patterns and processes, leadership, decision making, etc. Theoretical bases lie in social and organisational psychological communication theories.

(3) A laboratory for Human-Computer Interaction with hardware and software supporting synchronous and asynchronous communication tasks. This 'testbed' can be used to evaluate existing and new CSCW-systems.
Contact: J.H. Erik Andriessen.

ETH - the Swiss Federal Institute of Technology

ETH is working on the MultimETH project. The goal is to design and prototype a conferencing system that supports real-time multimedia (image, text and voice, but not video) communication between workstations in a highly distributed environment using internationally standardised protocols. The conferencing system focuses on distributed document processing. It provides facilities for supporting joint editing, administration of shared and private documents, voting and other aspects of conference management.

The ODA document model is used and has been extended to accommodate dynamic objects. A prototype has been developed on SUN workstations using the OSI ISODE protocol environment. A set of performance measurement tools supports the evaluation of the system architecture and its protocols.
Contact: Hannes P. Lubich.

GMD (Gesellschaft fur Mathematik und Datenverarbeitug)

At the beginning of 1989, GMD's Institute for Applied Information Technology reorganised its entire research into ten principal research projects with a planning horizon of 10 - 15 years. One of these is the "Assisting Computer (AC)" project being undertaken by a team of about 20 researchers. The AC project is working towards a vision of a new generation of support systems. An essential characteristic of the AC will be its support for cooperation.

At the focus of the research is the support of asynchronous collaboration in a broad variety of situations, ranging from official procedures to more informal ways of working together in teams and groups. Two principal research goals are being pursued:
- tailorability, i.e. the support system can be tailored to varying cooperative tasks on the basis of a common cooperation model and use of a coordination toolkit;
- organisational integrability, i.e. the system will utilize a distributed organisational knowledge base containing static structures as well as dynamic behaviour of the user organisation, thus allowing for an integration of collaboration support with organisational structures.
A first prototype of the system is planned for 1992.
Contact: Peter Hoschka.

Ispra - Joint Research Centre of CEC

CSCW research at Ispra is focused on 'enabling technologies' for supporting the use of multimedia real-time desktop conferencing by geographically dispersed users. The work builds on experience in developing and using ISPRA's DUAL backbone network which incorporates a mix of X.25, multicast and synchronisation features.

The main objective of the work is the identification of requirements for the services which may be offered by an 'intelligent computer communication network'. Such a network should, ideally, simplify the conferencing software architecture, reduce the amount of data traffic, and minimise communication delays in the network. Accordingly, proposals for the creation of some new protocols, and for the modification of existing ones, are being developed.

A pilot conferencing system based on networked Unix workstations has been developed. The management of the conferencing system is implemented in a distributed manner through the set of conferencing agent modules residing in the participating workstations.
Contact: Adriano Endrizzi.

Risoe National Laboratory

The Cognitive Systems Group is developing experimental CSCW systems in conjunction with theoretical studies and field studies of cooperative work in complex work domains.

The Group is currently involved in the ESPRIT Basic Research Action MOHAWC (Models of Human Activities in Work Context) which started in 1989. Within this project, the Group is developing a conceptual framework for the analysis of cooperative work and distributed decision making in complex work domains. The approach taken concieves cooperative arrangements as emerging distributed formations shaped dynamically by the requirements of the domain and the characteristics of the technical and human resources at hand.

In the complex and dynamic work settings encountered in real world cooperative settings, cooperative work relations are in a state of perennial change and renegotiation. Thus, designers of information systems for domains such as offices and integrated manufacturing are faced with the challenging problem of supporting exchange of information between decision makers who have a high degree of autonomy in their strategies and conceptualisations.

Risoe is also involved in the ESPRIT II ISEM (IT Support for Emergency Management) project which started in 1989. ISEM is developing an integrated information system capable of supporting complex, dynamic distributed decision making in the cooperative management of emergencies. The work is focused on defining a system architecture and on developing an Application Generator and tools to support the full system life cycle. The development is driven by requirements derived from on-site and off-site emergency organisations in the nuclear and chemical industries.
Contact: Kjeld Schmidt.

RSO

RSO was founded in 1974 and started to introduce sociotechnical analysis and design in Italy by re-shaping the Tavistock Institute's teachings in original ways, and by establishing action research principles along the lines of Kurt Lewin's work and socio-analysis.

Today RSO is a leader in the area of cooperation technologies (CT) in Italy. Besides offering consultancy and training in this field, RSO has also developed a methodology to design cooperative networks. The methodology's approach is based on the consonance of the organisational and technological environment. Cooperation is considered to be a fundamental phenomonenon in human work, and is analysed from its subject's point of view. Three main types of cooperation are identified:

(1) coordination - in which actions of individuals are synchronised;
(2) collaboration - people working together to perform a single task
(3) co-decision - actions that lead to a group decision.

RSO also founded the 'Laboratory for Cooperation Technologies' in 1988. This has the aim of observing, evaluating and testing cooperation technologies. A number of private and public Italian organisations subscribe to the Laboratory Programme which consists of seminars, workshops, study tours and product tests. **Contact:** Thomas Schael.

Swedish Institute of Computer Science (SICS)

SICS interest in CSCW includes models for cooperative work as well as the supporting distributed computer systems. SICS has a computer science perspective and cooperates with other groups having a behavioural science perspective such as KTH and SISU.

In the MultiG-program, a collaborative effort between academia and industry, research is being done on distributed multimedia applications in very high-speed networks. MultiG includes a CSCW project concerning cooperative system design in the telecom industry, with special emphasis on international standardisation of communication protocols. The end-users in this work process are peers, though they may have different experience and education. A mechanism for information sharing, the KnowledgeNet, is being developed and experimental studies of the end-users are being conducted. A distributed workstation environment, including videophone integrated with multi-user editors, simulators and other applications is being designed.

In another project, cooperative problem-solving at construction sites will be studied. In this work process end-users have different well-defined roles. A distributed mobile workstation environment (walkstations) with supporting applications will be developed. **Contact:** Bjorn Pehrson.

TA-Triumph-Adler

At Triumph-Adler the mobile PC line is considered to be of strategic importance. A complete solution is being researched including hardware, software and group productivity tools in order to respond to new market needs. Mobile PCs facilitate easy exchange of information using different kinds of networks such as public switched networks, LANs and WANs; while group productivity tools support asynchronous collaboration in the domain of

workgroup task management. The collaboration tools are being based on an Activity Coordination Model. Activities being focused on a range from highly structured to completely unstructured and represent the full spectrum of work which users are likely to have to undertake.
Contact: Klaus Kreplin.

Technical Research Centre of Finland

The Laboratory for information Processing started the DISSPRO project in 1988. The aim is to investigate management, communication and collaboration issues within the software development process. Two sets of requirements are being considered; one to support development work which is distributed between several distinct organisations; and the other to support collaboration between team members within a software development group. In the first case the problem areas are the terms and relations of sub-contracting, interfaces between organisation, communication between groups and management of the total effort. In the second case, tools for communication, cooperation, document sharing and circulation are required.

The project is developing the DISSGEN prototype generator (Distributed Software Engineering Environment Generator). DISSGEN will have the ability to generate various experimental distributed environments with selected tools supporting project management, communication and cooperation.
Contact: Sakari Kalliomaki.

Technical University of Aachen

CSCW research at Aachen focuses on knowledge-based support for distributed cooperation in co-authoring and software development. Within the ESPRIT II MULTIWORKS project a system called CoAUTHOR which supports the production of hypermedia documents by multiple authors, is being developed.

The process of authoring a hypermedia document is based on a tri-partite model. In the first phase (idea processing) the issues which have to be covered by the document are determined. In the second phase (document design) a formal document structure is set up and associated with the conceptual items from the idea processing phase. Finally, during document generation, ideas get implemented by appropriate hypermedia chunks.

The group level of co-authoring also has three major layers. Group work starts with the generation of individual contributions, such as ideas, outline proposals, and specific text portions. Each of the objects emerging from these phases is open for annotation by other group members. After collecting the group's conmments on individual contributions these units have to be combined according to the thematical and formal requirements of the whole document.

The first prototype of the CoAUTHOR System offers a client-server type architecture with three types of servers - a knowledge-based management server, a multimedia database server, and a real-time conferencing system facility for short-term communication management of group authoring. Two kinds of clients are offered - the Interaction Toolbox supporting hypermedia editors and browsers for the graphical mainipulation of multimedia objects and knowledge representation structures; and the Group Toolbox containing methodologies for voting, structured argumentation, management of authoring roles, access to external programs, etc.

In another project, "Expert Cooperation in Object Bases for Design Applications", a similar group model forms the basis for support within CASE environments. An experimental environment has been implemented which includes tools for design decision support (argumentation and multicriteria decision making), distributed design decision execution (contracting and contract monitoring), version and configuration management, and result integration (conflict handling). These group models and tools form part of the DAIDA environment (ESPRIT 892) for the development and maintenance of database-intensive software.

Contacts: Stefan Eherer and Matthias Jarke.

Technical University of Madrid

The Department of Telematic Systems Engineering (DIT) has been involved in several projects in the CSCW research field (AMIGO CACTUS, SECOM/SECNET). Work currently underway includes the PECOS project, an ESPRIT Exploratory Action. The first phase of PECOS involves CSCW background investigation and conceptual analysis and will produce proposals for modelling cooperative situations and for designing appropriate support tools. The second phase will evaluate the proposed modelling strategies by means of two case studies: co-working in project management and cooperative decision making in complex projects.

Another relevant project is GAUCHO (ESPRIT II) whose main objective is to provide an integrated environment for the use of OSI communication services by distributed applications. An architectural model has been defined and a system independent implementation is underway. In addition, GAUCHO will provide a general high level macro-service oriented towards the communication procedures required by distributed applications.

Other relevant work includes the modelling and prototype implementation over a LAN of distributed cooperative activities, and the design of highly functional user interfaces. The Department is also involved in the COST Co-Tech programme.

Contact: Encarna Pastor.

Technical University of Vienna

In January 1991 the department of Applied Computer Science started work on COTERM, a two-year interdisciplinary project with Social Scientists to develop principles and guidelines for ethical product development for CSCW applications. Empirical findings are being obtained from the problem domain of computer supported appointment and meeting arrangement. Conceptual and theoretical results will relate to software engineering techniques for CSCW applications (waterfall model, prototyping, user participation, design support), to knowledge representation, and to evaluation mechanisms for CSCW software.

Contacts: Brigitte Haberkorn and Christian Stary.

University of Aarhus

For almost two decades the Computer Science Department has been working on cooperative development of computer systems and on object-oriented languages, environments, and techniques. In 1990 a project was started that combines these two areas: the design of an open object-oriented environment that supports development of computer systems as a cooperative activity. Tools and "materials" for building a broad variety of systems, including groupware, are being built. Investigations are also being made into how to support end-user/developer cooperation by building application-specific tools and "materials".
Contact: Morten Kyng.

University of Amsterdam

Amsterdam's Centre for Innovation & Co-operative Technology is working on a project known as The Amsterdam Meeting Environment (AME). Based on networked Macintosh computers the AME is designed for large, face-to-face groups of up to 21 people who wish to deal collectively with an "externally structured problem". This is the type of issue for which there is no "correct solution", and whose boundaries depend on, and change with, the participants. Many issues in town and community planning, problems of the environment, and questions of design and organisation belong to this category. AME is an experimental facility designed to embody the following two central concepts.

(1) Double-level language. This rests on an analysis that successful computer supported interaction involves two levels of language. The first level is a "formal language". This has its own constraints/rules, and can be manipulated directly (for example, a model, a design, a text). All group members have access to this 'shared material'. The analogy is with two people carrying a table through a door. This means roughly that group members communicate implicitly through what they do to the material. My changes have consequences for your work, and vice versa. In a large group it is important to maintain the risk that each may change another's contribution - otherwise there is a tendency to "speak without listening". The second level is "dialogue language". At this level, group members talk about, interpret, negotiate, and coordinate their actions on the object at the first level.

(2) Caucus. This rests on the analysis that consensus is only one dimension of group process. Equally, or even more important, is the ability of the group to maintain variety and complexity. The term is taken from the political process of shifting coalitions and of behind the scenes talking and attempts to influence. It is believed that "caucusing" within a large group will maintain the collective ability to break consensus, to shift perspective, and to be unpredictable - properties of innovative approaches.

A network of microcomputers supports these processes by providing three levels of window onto the "shared material", plus the ability to talk about it. The first window level is the "public screen", the second provides caucus screens and the third provides individual screens.

AME is being developed as a face-to-face environment - with a small "e". The intention is not to develop a high-tech Meeting Room, but a set of human techniques that happen to work better with computer support; and that are useful in many different contexts, including meetings where not all the participants can be in the same place. **Contact:** Mike Robinson.

University College Dublin

The department of Computer Science is actively involved in two areas of CSCW: the development of collaborative business applications and the design, development and management of the infrastructural platforms to support CSCW applications. The department participated in the COST AMIGO project and is now involved in the Co-Tech programme.

The department's Computer Networks and Distributed Systems (CNDS) group is researching distributed network management (considered to be an increasingly important CSCW application candidate), and the technology issues of building the infrastructure platforms for CSCW-based systems. This group is involved in a national 'Applied Technology' initiative in the telecommunications area, working with industry on the take-up of telecommunications services and applications.

A second research area is that of collaborative IT support systems in business. The department is researching methods of analysis, design and evaluation for CSCW applications. The belief is that these methods should be collaborative, which leads to a second area of involvement - the development of groupware tools to support collaborative design and evaluation. Some collaborative evaluation instruments have been designed and prototypes are being developed. The department is actively seeking support to set up a groupware laboratory to develop and research business CSCW applications. **Contact:** Ahmed Patel, Michael Sherwood-Smith (only Michael Sherwood-Smith's address is included in Appendix D).

University of Geneva

Geneva's Centre Universitaire d'Informatique is interested in the cooperative nature of object-oriented software development. CSCW-related issues that have been addressed include the following:
- class management - the problems arising when large class collections are shared by large numbers of developers;
- design of a data model for software information which attempts to support cooperative work (flexible sharing of data, notification mechanisms);
- integration of versioning with hypertext in order to better support the sharing of hypertext webs.

Contact: Simon Gibbs.

University of Hohenheim

A computer supported meeting room environment called the Computer Aided Team Room (CATeam Room) is currently under development at the University of Hohenheim. CATeam is a collection of concepts and computer supported tools to improve group work productivity. Group work is considered to be a mix of phased tasks, any one of which can be accomplished by group members either meeting to work together or individual members working separately. Communication about task content and about how to solve problems (coordination) takes place continuously.

The CATeam Room is intended to provide a laboratory to research CATeam tools for both the meeting phase and for supporting distributed group work. The room can accomodate a maximum of 20 participants in a flexible configuration. It provides immediate access to personal computers which are linked by a local area network and which provide communication capabilities, a video network and access to large public screen displays.

The links between the collocated and distributed work phases, and the integration of remote meeting participants into the meeting phases are of major concern. Consequently the CATeam Room will eventually include video conferencing and computer conferencing (bulletin board) capabilities.

The CATeam Room will be used to research questions such as:
* how can teamwork be improved by the use of information technology (IT)?
* what changes in meetings are possible through IT use?
* what changes in meetings are necessary for IT use?
* that changes in meetings result from IT use?
* To what extent can results of empirical studies performed in the USA be applied to Europe and especially to Germany?
* do studies need to be replicated due to cultural differences?

The Hohenhein CATeam research group cooperates with other researchers in multi-criteria decision making, communication science, sociology and psychology, within the university.
Contacts: Helmut Krcmar and Henrik Lewe (only Helmut Krcmar's address is included in Appendix D).

University of Jyvaskyla

The Department of Computer Science and Information Systems is involved in CSCW research in two ways. It is studying various existing CSCW approaches and it has developed SAMPO - an approach to the design and development of communication-oriented CSCW applications. Frameworks have been developed with which to analyse existing CSCW approaches and technologies, and to identify areas in which CSCW applications are required.

In the SAMPO project, methods to analyse and design cooperative work settings are being developed. SAMPO's approach is based on speech act theory and it is oriented towards modelling the communication patterns in offices and other cooperative work environments. Current work deals with further development of the description methods and comparison of the SAMPO approach with other modelling approaches. Also prototypes of tools that support the description methods have been constructed.
Contact: Kalle Lyytinen.

University of Karlsruhe

Karlsruhe's Institute for Telematics and the University of Kaiserslautern's Telematics Working Group are collaborating in an effort to provide development and runtime support for cooperative applications in a distributed environment.

Research is aimed at realising a Group Interaction Environment (GroupIE), which supports interaction and coordination within spatially dispersed teams. Special emphasis is put on using distributed computer systems. Interactions, as the basic means of collaboration, have characteristics (for example, explicit/implicit, media type and degree of synchronism), which can be adapted to different qualities of the underlying communication subsystem. Coordination constraints can be specified based on task and team structures. Throughout the work the object-oriented paradigm is being pursued, and Smalltalk-80 implementations are under way.

This work is being validated in the field of Computer-Aided Instruction within NESTOR - a joint project of the Universities of Karlsruhe and Kaiserslautern and Digital Equipment Corporation. NESTOR is researching the support of authoring and learning in networked, multimedia environments. Teamwork of authors as well as learners is one important feature of this work.
Contact: Tom Ruedebusch.

University of Lund

CSCW work in the department of Information & Computer Science started with the SOFIA project in 1989. This was a joint project with the department of Psychology, which ended in Januray 1991. This line of research will continue to be explored in similar projects in the future in the department of Information & Computer Science.

The aim is to identify the types of computer support that will promote cooperation in the work place; and to assess how such computer support should be designed and applied so as to gain maximum benefit. The work is also investigating the impacts that different computer systems and applications have on work content, discretion, and learning.

A crucial issue is how new CSCW systems can be most effectively introduced into already established computer environments. Another concern is to establish CSCW's potential impact on, among other things, the learning and development of competence (eg. in collective decision making). A third concern is to study the significance of the organisational climate and culture on the development and use of CSCW systems.

Empirical investigations are being done using office and administrative work within public administration and private industry. Case-studies in which the impacts of commercially available cooperative support systems on existing tasks and operations, are also being observed.
Contact: Agneta Olerup.

University of Milano

In 1985 the Department of Computer Science started the CHAOS (Commitment Handling Active Office Systems) Project. CHAOS is based on the concept that language and speech can be equated to physical action, and that the commitments and responsibilities uttered in speech can be recorded in a knowledge base and used to structure subsequent mail-based communication within a group. For example, if a conversation agrees that an individual shall be responsible for all issues to do with UNIX, then all messages on the topic of UNIX are subsequently directed to that person.

The first small prototype, CHAOS-1, was completed in the spring of 1986 and was developed on a Vax 750, in Franz Lisp + Pearl. At the end of 1988 two further funded projects were obtained and are now supporting the development of two new prototypes. The first is within an Esprit-II Project, ITHACA (Integrated Toolkit for Highly Advanced Computer Applications), whose main partners are Nixdorf, Bull, University of Geneva and Datamont. Within this project the University of Milano is developing a User-To-User Communication Support mechanism to be integrated into the Office Environment that is being developed by the other partners.

In the second project (funded within the Italian National Research Council's GROUPWARE Subproject) the Department of Computer Science is collaborating with the Politecnico of Turin and the University of Trento, to develop the CHAOS-2 prototype.

The prototypes in both projects are being developed on a SUN 3/60 machine. In ITHACA, Lelisp and Bull's prototypal environment AMS (Activity Management System) are being used.

Two other CSCW research projects are also being conducted within the Department of Computer Science: in the first (the INFOKIT project), topics such as co-authoring and semi-structured communication in application engineering are being investigated; in the second (Stress impact of reliability of complex systems) cooperation patterns and cooperation support tools are being investigated from psychological and organisational points of view. **Contacts:** Fiorella De Cindio, Giorgio De Michelis, Carla Simone, Elsa Bignoli, Renata Tinini and Annamaria Zanaboni (only Giorgio De Michelis' address is included in Appendix D).

University of Roskilde

Roskilde's Department of Computer Science is working on consensus journals - a method of scientific communication that has the economy of invitational journals and the objectivity of journals based upon peer review. That is, all articles are published and the reader benefits from article selection based upon impartial refereeing. An additional benefit of consensus journals is that the negotiation process which typically occurs prior to publication, is automated, thus saving efforts of participants.

All readers are free to submit reviews that evaluate articles on a number of dimensions. A statistical procedure is used to identify the most knowledgeable representative of consensus positions and these referees are invited to submit articles that justify the review judgments they submitted. A major advantage of this approach is the ability to develop reputation without article publication.

The method includes a protection mechanism based upon pseudonyms which substitutes for the protection of anonymous review typical with scientific journals. This reduces the potential for irresponsible behaviour and facilitates reputation development. The level of quality enhancement is superior to that achievable with anonymous peer review.
Contact: David S. Stodolsky.

University of Stockholm

The Department of Psychology is doing a variety of CSCW-related work. The CAFKA project, being undertaken in conjunction with Linkoeping University's department of Computer Science, focuses on the way knowledge-based systems act as a communication mechanism between domain specialists and end-users. Questions about knowledge requirements for communication and tutoring, the interface requirements of knowledge based systems and the generation of verbal comments and explanations, are addressed theoretically and empirically. Several domains are being explored; chemistry, interface evaluation, medicine and home heating.

The AIDAI project is being undertaken with Uppsala University's Department of Computer Science. AIDAI aims to analyse communication difficulties between system designers and end-users. Tools for decreasing communication obstacles are being proposed and prototypes being developed and tested.

The programme "CAD/CAM with product models and AI", completed in 1990, developed outlines for systems supporting human problem solving at different phases of product design. In a similar vein, the Samtek project (being undertaken in conjunction with the Royal Institute of Technology, department of Manufacturing Systems) is analysing cooperation between mechanical designers and production planners to identify factors which contribute to failure and success in the design process. Requirements for computer support are being identified.
Contact: Yvonne Waern.

University of Trento

Trento's Computer Science Institute is working on group decision making, hypertext systems, organisational behaviour and the cooperative aspects of game theory. In the area of group decision making, a prototype cooperative work system is being developed, incorporating economic and organisational models of the environment under consideration, and models for consensus representation. In addition an investigation of 'support systems for group decision making in cooperative work' is being undertaken under the auspices of a 'Laboratory for Experimental Economics' - joint venture between the Computer Science Institute, the Economi Department of the Business Studies Institute and the Informatics Institute of the Economics Faculty. The Laboratory will also investigate organisational learning.

The aim of the game theory research is to set up, verify and apply some mathematical models of profit and cost sharing, using solutions suggested by the theory of cooperative games. It deals with cooperative game models relative to production, flow, marke queues, inheritance, bankcruptcy, route and ecology.

The hypertext work concentrates on using commercially available hypertext products to support the distance learning activities of a 'Specialised Post-diploma Computer School' conducted in Open University style. Initial use of the first prototypes has identified a variety of problems which are now being addressed. Use of the systems over a network is being trialed, and a procedure for the transfer of hypertexts from a Windows environment to an OS/2 environment is being developed.
Contact: Luisa Mich.

University of Twente

Twente's School of Management Studies is doing extensive research into the 'upstream' end of the software engineering process. The research is largely based on the modelling of organisations as systems of social norms (a norm can be thought of as kind of tacit legal rule). To apply information technology (IT) resources to such norms they have to be made explicit, as though they were the 'law' of the group. This entails three major components:

- the logical structure of the norm itself and the terms (and their semantics) used to express the norm. During semantic analysis group members explore what they mean by all the terms they use to describe the problem domain. The result is a very stable description of what the users perceive to exist in their world;
- the agent (person or process) responsible for the behaviour specified by the norm;
- the norm activation pattern dictated by internal and external events.

Automated support for the derivation and control of each component has been developed in a Norm Based Management System (NBMS). The norm-based architecture removes the dependency of application programs on knowledge of the business. However it demands a semantic database of exceptional stability in the face of organisational change. A normbase partitions application programmes into knowledge of the group (team, business, legal, social) norms and knowledge of how to exploit the given IT resources most effectively. The NBMS will be a tool used on a day-to-day basis by group members to develop their group knowledge and to carry out and redefine their responsibilities.

To support this work the NBMS team is collaborating with the Finnish SAMPO speech act programme, and with the University of Texas in Austin to investigate conversational processes in EDI systems for negotiating international contracts. It is also participating in the Co-Tech IT Support for Group Knowledge Development project.
Contacts: Ronald Stamper and Kees van Slooten (only Ronald Stamper's address is included in Appendix D).

B.8 North American CSCW Research

Some of the organisations undertaking CSCW research in North American are listed below. Note that inclusion of an organisation in the list does not necessarily mean that all the CSCW work being undertaken within its confines is included.

Bellcore

Bellcore is doing a wide variety of CSCW-related work, one example being in the field of software development (the ICICLE project), and another example being in the use of video technology (the VideoWindow project).

ICICLE investigated the process of formal code inspection, and developed software to support discussion of the code prior to inspection meetings, and to assist in finalising inspectors' comments during face-to-face meetings. The VideoWindow project explored the possibility of extending a shared space over a considerable distance without impairing the quality of interactions among users or requiring any special actions to establish a conversation. This possibility was investigated by installing large video windows, around 3 feet high and 8 feet wide, in two rooms in a building. People in those rooms could see and hear what was going on in the other room through the video window.

Both projects reflect Bellcore's general interest in exploring the use of both formal and informal communications as mechanisms for coordinating the social and production roles of people in the workplace.

Contacts: Laurence Brothers and Robert Kraut.

Digital Equipment Corporation (DEC)

Since the mid-1980s DEC has been developing coordination systems to support the software development process. More recently it has been researching the provision of support for group meetings, and in particular the way in which proven organisational effectiveness techniques can be combined with existing computer technology. The aim is to create an environment that promotes and supports group performance and increases group focus. On the basis of this research DEC now provides a consulting service called Meetings-that-Work™. The service offers an integrated computer-supported solution for improving the productivity and effectiveness of collaborative work. It can be used, for example, to create computer-supported meetings for real-time, distributed teams.

Contact: David Marca.

Florida International University

The School of Computer Science is undertaking the COMDEC (COMmunication in DECision Making) project to elaborate and model communication in collaborative environments. Its objectives are to investigate the role of communication among collaborative agents according to decision making models, and to model decision making based on communicating agents. Approaches from several disciplines (CSCW, AI, HCI) have been reviewed and a conceptual model has been developed and is being formalised.

Contact: Christian Stary.

Hewlett-Packard Laboratories;, Palo Alto

HP Laboratories is researching the management of computer-based conversations in work groups through technologies that enable teams to capture and structure discourse. This is useful for work groups engaged in specialised, recurring conversations, where building specific conversational structures for certain tasks allows them to coordinate their activities more effectively.

To support such conversations, the Strudel system was developed. Strudel embraces the paradigms of semi-structured messages, active messages and conversation management, within a simple model of task and action. Strudel provides email users with the ability to define their messages as 'conversation moves' (for example, a request to repair a defect), and to specify 'actions' (either a text definition of things to be done or an automatic event initiated in another application program) and 'action items' (memos describing an activity the user intends to carry out, and the activity status).

Strudel differs from previous approaches in that users can dynamically evolve conversation moves in the course of dealing with mail. However, this pragmatic 'local management' can also be interleaved with predefined 'globally managed' conversations. Another important feature of this work is its commitment to interoperability between different email systems. Hence Strudel has been designed to enable a user to accept, and deal with conventional unstructured email, as well as email from other conversation management, active message or coordination systems. The Strudel team is actively seeking cooperation with developers of such systems to try out interoperability in practice.

HP Labs is also researching the role of multimedia computer systems in the communication, collaboration, and information sharing activities of physically and temporally distributed workgroups. Some media, such as full motion video, are very expensive, not only in terms of media specific hardware, but also in storage and communications costs. Research is being done on solutions that reduce hardware costs and optimize added value. A hardware peripheral to be attached to a PC or workstation to provide a media subsystem, is being designed; and a network-transparent media management toolkit for controlling and manipulating the media subsystem is being developed.The goal is to make media accessible at reasonable cost for application developers.
Contacts: Walt Hill, Audrey Ishikazi, Allan Kuchinsky, Bob Leichner, Niels Mayer, Allan Shepherd (only Allan Kuchinsky's address is included in Appendix D).

Institute for the Future (IFTF)

IFTF is an independent non-profit research group which carries out applied research supported primarily by private corporations. IFTF has two major projects in the CSCW area. One - Outlook - focuses on CSCW market trends, including competitive information, sales trends and forecasts. The other - the Groupware Users' Project - is supported by a group of non-competing user organisations, all of whom are exploring some aspect of CSCW use. IFTF conducts research on their early field experiences and facilitates exchanges among the companies.

In addition to these two projects, IFTF undertakes special projects and writing relating to CSCW (for example, the books on 'Groupware' and 'Leading Business Teams' - see Appendix C).
Contacts: Bob Johansen, Paul Saffo, Robert Mittman and Alexia Martin (only Bob Johansen's address is provided in Appendix B).

Massachusetts Institute of Technology

The MIT Center for Coordination Science conducts multidisciplinary research to understand how new kinds of technology can help people work together more effectively. Some Center projects focus on studying how people work together now and analysing how they might do so differently with new kinds of systems. For instance, recent projects have studied engineering change processes in manufacturing organisations and customer support "hot lines" in software companies.

Other projects focus on developing new collaborative tools for such tasks as group information sharing, making group decisions, and managing projects. Recent projects have included developing Information Lens (an intelligent mail sorting tool), Object Lens (a "radically tailorable" tool for many kinds of collaborative work), Answer Garden (a tool for growing organisational memories by capturing the answers to commonly asked questions), and HyperVoice (a telephone-based interface for voice databases).

Finally, some projects focus on developing new theories of coordination on the basis of which more effective coordination systems can be built. For instance, recent work has developed new formalisms for representing coordination processes and for cataloging generic coordination processes.
Contact: Thomas W. Malone.

Microelectronics and Computer Technology Corporation (MCC)

MCC is a cooperative research enterprise whose mission is to strengthen and sustain North America's competitiveness in IT. Participating organisations that are normally fierce marketplace competitiors join MCC to leverage their research dollars and minimize the risks of long-term research. Within MCC's Software Technology Program, several projects have been carried out under the heading of Team Technologies. The overall goal of these projects is to improve software product quality by improving the productivity of large teams of product designers and developers. The earliest work focused on improving meeting productivity. Project Nick used a novel combination of technologies to support people working on unstructured problems in face-to-face meetings. This work led naturally to exploration of technologies to support groups where the members were distributed rather than collocated. Another early project developed GROVE, a real-time, multi-user outline editor that demonstrated how concurrent editing can be productive for synchronous, distributed group interaction.

The gIBIS, Germ, and rIBIS work explored the use of issue-based information systems to support design teams in documenting the rationale of their system designs. gIBIS was the first IBIS-based tool. Germ is a generalization of gIBIS with a user-defined schema allowing the tool to support hypertext structures. rIBIS was a real-time version of Germ that supported user interactions in both tightly coupled (highly focused group work) and loosely coupled (parallel individual activity) modes.

The Coordination Theory and Technology Project is the current focus of MCC's CSCW research, and is developing a software system to support coordination among people tasks, and resources in an organisation. The system is grounded in a formal model of coordination based on organisational role theory, and provides a distributed environment for the planning, enactment, status monitoring, and dynamic reconfiguration of organisational activities. The research is making use of the results of case studies of the coordination phenomenon in MCC shareholder settings.
Contacts: Baldev Singh, Gail Rein (only Gail Rein's address is included in Appendix D).

Queen's University

The School of Business has been studying the effects of using group decision support systems (GDSS) on group processes and outcomes, since the mid-1980s. The work has focused primarily on face-to-face electronic meeting environments and has mainly used two GDSSs; DECAID1 and GroupSystems. A number of research projects have been completed including a longitudinal study of the same groups using the GDSS' over 2 years, and a series of studies into electronic brainstorming.
Contact: Brent Gallupe.

University of British Columbia

CSCW research at UBC focuses on the examination of behavioural effects of computer-mediated group interactions; and on the design of interfaces for cooperative work. Examination of behavioural effects is being undertaken with reference to decision making and problem solving groups. Effects being studied at the individual and group levels include the committment of participants to decisions made using CSCW technologies, and the re-distribution of influence among the power bases in a group. At the organisational level, the adaptive changes that have to occur to accommodate CSCW technologies, and the structural changes that take place in an organisation as the use of CSCW grows, are being investigated.

The premise of the research into interfaces is that some of the interface needs for cooperative work are different from the needs of the single user human-computer interaction. UBC intends to identify the differences, to develop the interfaces to accommodate the new needs and to test the interfaces empirically.

The building of a Group Decision Systems Support laboratory started in 1990. The laboratory's main purpose is to perform experimental studies to build and test theories related to the effects of using such technologies. The laboratory is centered around a 'decision room'. Each participant is provided with a computer and requisite software. A public display facility is also available. The entire system is networked so participants can communicate with each other over the network, and can display pertinent information on the public display. The facilities will also have outer rooms with computers, which can be included in the network.
Contact: Srinivasan (Chino) Rao.

University of Calgary

The department of Computer Science is investigating the sharing of applications, the use of group sketching and drawing tools, asynchronous group writing and the integration of conventional electronic mailwith repertory grid elicitation.

A prototype system called Share has been built to enable participants of a real-time distributed meeting to share applications via a 'shared window'. Users see the same image of the running application on their own screens and interact with it by taking turns. While Share allows any unaltered single-user application to be brought into a meeting, the multi-user nature of the work is transparent to the application itself. Share's functionality includes registering users, maintaining consistent shared views, managing floor control for serial input to applications, and allowing attendees to gesture and annotate around the view. New insights have been obtained by decoupling the view-sharing kernel from the floor control interface.

For group sketching research the GroupSketch tool has been built. This allows a small geographically distributed group to list, draw, and gesture in a communal work surface with large unique cursors visible on all displays. Observations of design sessions indicate that people use GroupSketch in much the same way as they use face to face communal sketchpads. The lessons learnt are now being applied to GroupDraw, an object-based drawing package providing multi-user access to selectable objects (lines, rectangles, text, etc.).

For the group writing research the department has developed GroupWriter, a Macintosh-based writing tool that supports asynchronous group-writing. It relies on version control and on annotation support. Changes to a document are tracked by the system, and writers can attach notes to their work.

Finally, repertory grid research is using RepGrid-Net, a computer-based message system that integrates electronic mail and bulletin board facilities with repertory grid elicitation and analysis facilities. Similarities between participant's grids are analysed to provide a socionet of people with common viewpoints, and this may be used to access the mail system to communicate with them.
Contact: Saul Greenberg.

University of Georgia

The Department of Management has a computer-augmented teamwork project under the general umbrella of its Executive 2000 program. The project has six research themes: comparison of team technologies, facilitation and leadership, team development, team creativity, cross-cultural analysis, and adoption and diffusion of team technology. Four team technologies are installed: SAGE, OptionFinder, VisionQuest and GroupSystems. Two laboratories are equipped with large screen projectors and networked personal computers. Studies completed or in progress include thhe following:
- experimental laboratory research comparing decision making using different implementations of the team technology concept;
- field research on the adoption, diffusion, and use of a keypad based system;
- experimental laboratory research on the impact of team technology on decision making under stress, and stress induced by team technology;
- decision making by dyads communicating via face-to-face, audio, and electronic mail;
- investigation of team technology use in different national cultures;
- development of a training program for facilitating computer-augmented teams;
- joint development with the National University of Singapore of a Macintosh-based group decision support system.

The project researchers maintain an extensive network of relationships with organisations and individuals working in the area of computer-augmented teamwork. Demonstrations of, and training in, different team technologies have been conducted for a wide variety of US organisations.
Contacts: Bob Bostrom, David Van Over, and Rick Watson (only Rick Watson's address is provided in Appendix B).

University of Houston

The Information Systems Research Center in Houston's College of Business Administration is conducting a critical review of CSCW literature and ongoing research; a survey of the use of groupware in industry and government in Houston; and research into group decision support systems using the VisionQuest tool.

The CSCW review is being done in order to develop a theoretical framework for the CSCW field, and to identify relevant underlying themes. The review is considering group work in special environments (such as advanced meeting rooms), and group work supported by software embedded in the work environment (such as electronic mail, action tracking and co-authoring software).

The survey of groupware use is being based on a sample of 75 firms in Houston (25 small firms selected randomly, 25 large firms selected randomly and 25 firms that sponsor the Information Systems Research Center). For the survey, Groupware is defined as a software application which recognizes the existence of a group and permits two-way communication between its members.

The application areas are defined by one major dimension and two sub-dimensions. The major dimension is 'face-to-face' *vs* 'dispersed work'. The sub-dimensions are 'degree of electronic support' and 'synchronicity - synchronous or asynchronous'. **Contact:** Rudy Hirschheim.

University of Michigan

The Cognitive Science & Machine Intelligence Laboratory (CSMIL) conducts research on a variety of topics in CSCW. Much of the current work focuses on synchronous collaboration, both face-to-face and distributed, and is a mixture of field studies and laboratory research The main application domain is software engineering, especially the early design stages. A shared editor called ShrEdit is used in many of these studies, though other groupware systems are also being investigated. Work has also begun on how a combination of video (either analog or digital) and groupware tools can be used to support distributed work. The Collaboration Technology Suite (CTS) is a special research facility for this work. Several corporate partners are collaborators in the research. **Contact:** Gary Olson.

University of Oakland

Oakland's School of Business Administration is involved in several CSCW-related projects including the following:
- TOOLCRIB; an ongoing project which started in 1987, studying CSCW in small business environments. The purpose of the project is to develop software tools for CSCW system construction in settings where a variety of business documents must be handled by multiple users in accordance with electronic data interchange (EDI) standards.
- POGO; the development of a program for the ordering of group opinions. POGO supports the asynchronous user expansion of ideas on chosen topics; the offering of comments on previously submitted ideas; and the rating of ideas by users. POGO is intended to be a component of a variety of larger systems.
- IMS; a study of the management problems associated with integrated manufacturing systems, and the potential uses of CSCW in their solution. Major problems include the need for extensive new language learning, the replacement of 'feel' by symbolic representations, major changes in the structure of management, and the alteration of the constraints that existed before the implementation began.
 Contact: Robbin R. Hough.

University of Texas

The Laboratory for Organisational Computing (LOC) is researching organisational forms, tasks and processes, and is building groupware support for specific application requirements. The

93

Laboratory's work is based on an 'organizational computing development environment' (OCDE) which will support the modelling, creation, and experimentation of organisational forms, tasks and processes; and which will provide a library of services in the form of re-usable software objects which can be used to build a variety of applications for the organisation of tomorrow.

Several research projects, centered around the development of the LOC and the OCDE, are being conducted. The projects address one of three levels of organisational computing: the organisational level, the application level and the network level. The organisational level of the OCDE involves modelling and understanding the effects of organisational activities when they are distributed over space, time and people. Thus at this level, the behavioural properties of organisational actions and their consequences is being studied.

The group application research looks at specific applications that can be built using the OCDE. It is anticipated that it is in specific end-user systems, rather than general functional tools, that groupware based systems and distributed applications will have their greatest pay-off. The research at the network level focuses on how to better utilize networks from an economic and managerial point of view. **Contact:** Andrew Whinston.

University of Toronto

Toronto's Computer Science Department is undertaking the CAVECAT project (Computer Audio Video Enhanced Collaboration And Telepresence). This is developing multi-modal communication support between personal workstations to enhance collaboration on complex work projects that take place at a distance (for example, software development, office work, management decision making, financial planning, medical diagnosis, medical consulting, etc.).

Existing research has demonstrated the insufficiency of voice and electronic communications for sustained and efficient collaboration. CAVECAT includes video in the communication, not just as a visual record of the collaboration communication, but as a manipulable user-managed object. The project team believes that by integrating video with the computer communication and control, and by improving the tools and the user interface for the computer and video portion of the communication, then it may be possible to undertake continued collaboration on complex work projects without requiring face-to-face communication. No communication technology has yet been developed which achieves this aim.

The research has two parts. The first integrates the video images into the window environment of personal workstations, and develops appropriate tools for the users of this arrangement. In the second part psychological and sociological studies of the work patterns that occur when using various tool options, are being carried out. These studies support the redesign of the system and evaluate its effectiveness as a communication interface. **Contact:** Marilyn Mantei.

Xerox Palo Alto Research Centre (PARC)

PARC has several ongoing research projects that investigate work practices and technologies to support group activity. Technologies include software and hardware for shared information (editing, drawing and hypermedia, for example) and video, audio, and computing networks for connecting people across space and time. In addition to exploring the use of these research technologies, studies of work practice focus on the social and technological structuring of everyday work activities in specific settings, and the relationship of empirical studies of current practice as a resource for design. **Contact:** Lucy Suchman.

B.9 CSCW research elsewhere in the world

Some of the organisations undertaking CSCW research outside Europe and North America are listed below. Note that inclusion of an organisation in the list does not necessarily mean that all the CSCW work being undertaken within its confines is included.

National Chiao Tung University (NCTU)

CSCW research at NCTU addresses four main areas: coordination theory, human-computer networks, organisational structures and coordination technology. Applied research projects include intelligent folders, subway coordinating system, and graphic coordination languages. The aim of the work is to identify optimal organisation and computing structures based on coordination technologies and coordination modes. **Contact:** Keh-Chiang Yu.

National University of Singapore

Research suggests that there are cross-cultural differences among nationals and that these differences have important implications for group behaviour and organisational behaviour. As group decision support system (GDSS) technology has a direct impact on the communication patterns of groups of people, a theory of GDSS may have to incorporate cultural factors. Most GDSS research up to 1988 was carried out in the individualistic culture of the USA with American subjects. The applicability of the findings of this research in collectivistic Asia-Pacific cultures, for example the Singaporean culture, was unknown. Research in GDSS at the Department of Information Systems and Computer Science (DISCS) was initiated to fill this gap in GDSS research.

The main goal of the DISCS' GDSS research project is to study the influence of cross-cultural differences among nationals on GDSS theory and design, and to develop a GDSS suited for use in collectivistic Asia-Pacific cultures. The aims of the project are:
- to set up a GDSS research facility at DISCS and acquire and instal GDSS software from GDSS research centres in the USA (the University of Minnesota SAMM software is being used);
- to conduct experiments with Singaporean groups and to study the impact of GDSS on group process and group outcomes;
- to compare the results of these experiments with the results of similar experiments in the USA and other countries, and identify the influence of cultural factors;
- to use the empirical results to review the GDSS theories and GDSS designs developed in the USA and adapt these to the Singaporean culture;
- to develop GDSS software using the theoretical concepts and design principles developed in this research (Macintosh-based SAGE software has been developed);
- to introduce GDSS to group decision making in public bodies, and government and business organisations in Singapore;

- to cooperate and collaborate with GDSS researchers in other countries in all aspects of this research;
- to develop a Chinese language GDSS (long-term goal).

Contacts: K.S.Raman, K. K. Wei (only K.S. Raman's address appears in Appendix D).

NTT

NTT is actively involved in basic and applied R&D to create a new age of telecommunication services based on an Integrated Services Digital Network (ISDN). NTT believes that human interface technologies will play a crucial role in making communication and computer technologies more easy-to-use and more effective in augmenting human abilities to think and share ideas. Since 1987, Human Interface Laboratories (HI Lab) have researched human interface technologies to create the next generation ISDN terminals and to investigate the nature of human communication. At present, 250 researchers are working in the HI Lab.

Communication has long been interpreted as electronic tele-communication in a physical sense. NTT believes that a higher view of communication should be taken: that it should be considered as inter-personal communication (or human-human interaction) that cannot be captured by the framework of the ISO seven layer communication model. Consequently, NTT considers "Human Interface" from the following two points of view: Human-Computer Interaction (HCI), and Human-Human Interaction (HHI).

HHI will enhance social productivity by providing electronically supported common workspaces that are both powerful and user-friendly. First, NTT is seeking to improve the HCI by using multi-media information processing technologies such as the recognition and synthesis of speech, images and words. Second, NTT is broadening the communication bandwidth of HHI over distance and over time. Third, much research is being done to analyse work and computer usability from the cognitive point of view.

In the second context (HHI), NTT is conducting a variety of CSCW research projects including:
- Visual TeleConsulting System: A teleconsulting system using face-to-face communication links and shared visual databases;
- TeamWorkStation: A cooperative work environment that provides open shared drawing space and face-to-face conversation links among distributed group members;
- Multimedia Teleconference System: A multimedia teleconferencing system that provides a common visual space for widely separated conferees.

Contact: Hiroshi Ishii.

Appendix C   Glossary

Abbreviations used within the text

ACB	Advanced Concepts Branch
ACE	Advanced communication experiments
ACM	Association of Computing Machinery
ATP	Advanced Technology Programme
CD-ROM	Compact disc - read-only memory
CSC	Computer Sciences Corporation
CSCW	Computer supported cooperative work
DP	Data processing
DVC	Desktop video conferencing
ECC	European Community Commission
EEC	European Economic Community
ESRC	Economic and Social Research Council
GDSS	Group decision support system
GWDP	Group work design procedure
IBC	Integrated broadband communications
IPSE	Integrated project support environment
ISDN	Integrated services digital network
IS	Information systems
IT	Information technology
LAN	Local area network
MECU	Millions of European currency units
MRC	Medical Research Council
NSF	National Science Foundation
OIS	Office information systems
OS	Open systems
OSI	Open systems interconnection
PC	Personal computer
RACE	Research and Development in Advanced Communications
R&D	Research and development
SERC	Science and Engineering Research Council
SIG	Special interest group
WAN	Wide area network

Terms used within the text

Activity processors: are computer programmes which support the organised and structured activity of groups by means of activity 'scripts' for each participant. The scripts, which may be predetermined or created/ modified mid-activity, enable the system to route information to appropriate people, to remind individuals of tasks that have fallen due and to provide information about the status of the activity. Activity processors are a more general form of procedure processing in that they do not constrain input to forms, and in that they enable more flexible, conversation-type interaction to be undertaken.

Advanced meeting room systems: see Meeting room systems.

Anthropology: the study of mankind; its origins, institutions, customs, religious beliefs, social relationships, etc.

Argumentation tools: enable members of a group to make their views explicit and to discuss them in a structured way. Such tools are often based on Issue-based Information Systems in which people can describe an issue, can identify positions relating to that issue, and can outline arguments for and against each position.

Asynchronous: occurring at different times.

Back projection systems: enable computer displays, overhead projector slides, 35 mm slides or video films to be projected from behind onto a large wall screen.

Bandwidth: the amount of data that can be transmitted by a communication channel - usually measured in bits per second.

Brainstorming: a structured problem solving or knowledge generation process consisting of, first, the uninhibited generation of ideas, and then the categorisation, synthesis and evaluation of those ideas.

Calendar systems: provide individuals in a group with their own diaries of activities and events, and with the ability to view the public parts of other people's diaries. Support is often provided to establish suitable meeting dates and to book agreed dates in the diaries of all concerned.

Co-authoring systems: support some or all aspects of the creation of documents by two or more people. This might include support for the initial development of ideas, for the establishment of an outline framework of the document, for the creation of text, for peer review and for version control.

Cognitive psychology: a field of study which addresses the dynamic role of cognitive processes, and which places a special emphasis on 'knowing' and 'perceiving' as contrasted with simple associative learning.

Collaboration research: research into the way in which two or more people collaborate together on one or more specific tasks.

Collaboratory: a term used originally in a USA National Science Foundation workshop [56] to describe a vision of a virtual electronic research center without walls, enabling thousands of researchers in hundreds of different geographically dispersed establishments, to collaborate together. The Collaboratory would provide a full range of services (such as a digital library), communication mechanisms (such as high resolution desktop video conferencing) and CSCW tools to encourage and augment the collaborative process.

Commitment making: the process whereby humans agree to undertake a task or to take on some responsibility.

Compression technology: equipment and systems designed to minimise the number of bits required to represent a given amount of information, in a reversible manner.

Computer conferencing systems: are more structured versions of simple electronic mail systems: instead of messages being sent to one or more individuals, they are sent to 'activities' or 'conferences' or bulletin boards'. Users become members of specific conferences and upon selecting a conference are presented with all new material that they have not yet seen. Individuals can simply read the contents of conferences or reply to particular messages if they so wish. All messages and replies are held in an ordered way within the conference and in this way 'conversations' are built up and can be reviewed as necessary.

Computer aided teams: groups of people working together supported by methods and by information and communication technology, based on insights into the human group working process.

Computer supported cooperative work: a generic term which combines the understanding of the way people work in groups with the enabling technologies of computer networking and associated hardware, software, services and techniques.

Coordination technology: information and communication systems, based on insights into how humans coordinate and collaborate, designed to improve the effectiveness of groups in organisations.

Coordination theory: a body of principles about how activities can be coordinated, that is, about how actors can work together harmoniously[57].

Co-Tech: The CSCW research programme being run within COST - a framework for cooperation in science and technology between European Community countries and other countries in Europe. COST programmes typically run for three years or more and provide funding for the travel and subsistence costs of meetings and exchanges of the participants. Participants are expected to make their own arrangements through their national bodies to cover the time and materials expenses of COST projects.

Decision support systems: see Group decision support systems.

Desktop conferencing: the use of a shared screen of information, together with an integrated voice link, by two or more people to undertake one or more specific tasks.

Desktop video conferencing: the use of a shared screen of information and an integrated voice and video link, by two or more people to undertake one or more specific tasks.

Discourse analysis: the recording and analysis of human conversations to understand how humans communicate.

Distance learning: facilities that enable students to undertake an educational course without having to attend the premises of the administering institution.

Electronic mail systems: enable messages to be sent to one or more people. The messages are delivered to an electronic mailbox and are accessed and read at the time and location of the recipients choosing.

ESPRIT: is the European Strategic Programme for Research & Development in Information Technologies. ESPRIT is funded by the European Community and administered by the European Commission.

Group activity support systems: provide computer support for specific group processes or activities (for example, idea generation, voting, prioritisation, strategic planning).

Group decision support systems (GDSS): interactive computer-based systems which facilitate the solution of unstructured problems by a set of decision makers working together as a group[6].

Group dynamics aspects: issues relating to the behaviour of individuals in groups, and the overall behaviour of the group itself.

Group process aspects: the human issues relating to the way people work in groups, and to the design of group work and associated computer support.

Groupware: a generic term for specialised computer aids that are designed for the use of collaborative work groups. Typically, these groups are small project-oriented teams that have important tasks and tight deadlines. Groupware can involve software, hardware, services, and/or group process support[2].

Group work design procedures: procedures and guidelines to support the process of analysing group work, the process of establishing alternative options for change, and the process of implementing a selected option.

High bandwidth networks: networks which support transmission rates in the order of millions of bits per second per channel.

High resolution: describes a display screen which has a very clear and sharp picture due to the very large number of individual dots (or pixels as they are known) with which the picture is made up.

Human factors: the scientific study of the relationship between people and their occupations.

Human interface: all aspects of the way people interact with computers including hardware, ergonomics, screen-based user interfaces and the design of jobs.

Hypertext systems: are a type of database which enable information to be held in chunks and for each chunk to be linked to other chunks. In this way a 'standard' route through the information can be provided. Individuals are able to create their own routes, and to add their own information (designated as either public or private material).

IPSE (Integrated Project Support Environment): a set of automated tools to support the software engineering process.

ISDN (Integrated Services Digital Network): a network allowing end-to-end digital connectivity thus permitting the transmission of data, voice and image on a common medium through a standardised set of common interfaces.

Juke box systems: systems supporting the physical storage, selection and playing of multiple discs (for example, optical discs).

Large wall screens: see wall screens.

Linguistics: the scientific study of language.

Local area network (LAN): a network of computing devices within one building, or a number of buildings in a specific geographical area, which does not rely on public services for interconnection of its various parts.

Meeting room systems: a range of computing hardware and software, and other systems, which support all aspects of face-to-face meetings, including the presentation of images on public screens, the structuring of meeting tasks such as brainstorming and prioritisation, and the recording of actions and minutes.

Multimedia: the combination of static/moving images, text and sound to form a composite medium. Computer-based multimedia facilities support the creation and manipulation of the individual and combined elements.

Naming tools: computer software which helps groups to agree on names for objects and concepts, and to record their existence and definitions.

On-line databases: repositories of information available via a network.

Open systems: systems whose ability to communicate and/or interwork, is standardised.

Organisation design: the process of analysing aspects of the structure and operation of an organisation, identifying options for design or change, and implementing selected designs or changes.

Organisation theory: the study of the structure, functioning and performance of organisations, and the behaviour of groups and individuals within them[58].

Pragmatics: a scientific field of study which attempts to understand the relationship between language and context.

Presentation packages: computer software designed to support the creation of textual, graphical, and multimedia material for display to an audience in the course of a presentation.

Procedure processing systems: enable electronic forms to be sent on predefined routes of people and roles, collecting specified information and alternating routes according to the inputs made. Reminders and status reports can be automatically produced.

Psychology: the science that studies behaviour and mental processes[59].

Prototyping: the creation and evaluation of test systems with the intention of identifying areas in which improvement and redesign is required (see also Usability Testing).

Quality circle: an organisational arrangement whereby groups of workers and managers meet and work together to improve the production process, the quality of products and the communication between workers and management.

RACE (Research and Development in Advanced Communications technologies in Europe): is part of the European Community's Framework Programme of collaborative research and development. RACE is focused on the development of advanced communications technology for the introduction of commercial Integrated Broadband Communications (IBC) services in Europe in 1995.

Remote screen sharing: see screen sharing systems.

Resolution: the characters and images on a display screen are formed from a collection of small dots. The number, spacing and size of the dots that are used to build up a computer screen display dictate how clear and sharp the display appears to the user. Although the number, size and spacing of dots all contribute to the resolution of the display, often only the number of dots vertically and horizontally (400 x 680 for example) is quoted as a measure of a screen's resolution.

Screen sharing systems: enable people using their own personal computer to see, and sometimes manipulate what is on other computer screens - be they in the same building connected via a local area network, or in a remote location connected via a phone line or other wide area network.

Shared databases: collections of information useful to members of a group, and accessible by all members of the group.

Shared filing systems: see shared databases.

Shared information systems: support the input, storage, navigation and retrieval of shared information by all members of a group.

Shared work space systems: enable members of a group to work together on common information or on a common writing and/or drawing surface.

Signal compression: the use of algorithms to reduce the amount of data necessary to transmit a given amount of information, thereby saving bandwidth.

Social psychology: a field of study dealing with social interaction and the ways in which individuals influence one another[59].

Sociology: a field of study dealing with group life and social organisation in literate societies

Software development: the process of designing and implementing computer software.

Software engineering: the application of engineering principles and practices to the analysis, design and implementation of computer software systems

Speech act theory: the common understanding of "taking action" is of someone doing something which can be seen, for example, moving or turning a steering wheel or making a photocopy or handing over a letter of resignation. The central insight of Speech Act theory is that just *to say something* - or more generally, to communicate something - *is also an act in its own right.*

Synchronous: occurring at the same time.

Technology for teams: information and communication systems and associated methods of working, built around insights into the human group working process and designed to improve the effectiveness of group work.

Usability testing: the systematic evaluation of an object, system or procedure, under near real-world conditions, with the intention of identifying areas in which improvement and redesign is required to ensure ease of use.

User involvement: the discussion, analysis, design, prototyping and implementation of systems with the direct involvement of the people who will use those systems.

Value added network services (VANS): (sometimes known as Value Added Data Services - VADS) access to host-based services provided by a network service supplier; for example, electronic data interchange, on-line databases, electronic mail and directory services.

Video compression: the use of algorithms to reduce the amount of data needed to transmit a given amount of video information, thereby saving bandwidth.

Video conferencing: systems which allow two or more people in separate rooms, buildings or geographical regions, to interact while both seeing and hearing each other.

Wall screens: large public display screens on which computer screen displays, overhead projector slides, 35 mm slides, static or moving video images, etc. can be presented for viewing by an audience.

Wide area network (WAN): a network of computing devices located in different geographical locations interconnected usually by public communication services.

Workgroup computing: activities undertaken on a network using software application programmes designed to support the members of a group.

Workplace design: the design of all aspects of a workplace in relation to the use of computer systems by its occupants. workplace design issues include workstation design, lighting, room climate, noise, room layout and on-going upkeep and maintenance of the workplace and its contents.

Workstation video: see Desktop video conferencing.

X.400: a series of standards defining the functionality of message handling systems and their interconnection.

X.500: a series of standards defining the functionality and interconnection of Directories containing information about the users of message handling systems and other related information.

Appendix D   Useful Addresses and Contacts

Ablex Publishing Corporation, 355 Chestnut St., Norwood, NJ 07648-9975, USA.
Tel: +1-201-767-8450   Fax: +1-201-767-6717

Academic Press Limited, Foots Cray, Sidcup, Kent, DA14 5HP, UK.
Tel: +44-81-300-0155   Fax: +44-81-309-0807

ACM, 11 West 42nd Street, New York, NY 10036, USA.
Tel: +1-212-869-7440   Fax: +1-212-944-1318
Email: acmember@acmvm.bitnet

Advanced Concepts Branch, (CCTA), CCTA, Riverwalk House, Millbank, London,
SW1P4RT, UK.
Tel: +44-71-217-3049   Fax: +44-71-217-3449

Andersen, Verner, Risoe National Laboratory, PO Box 49, DK-400 Roskilde, Denmark.
Tel: +45-2-371-212   Fax: +45-2-373-993

Anderson, Bob, Rank Xerox EuroPARC, 61 Regent Street, Cambridge, CB2 1AB, UK.
Tel: +44-223-341-500   Fax: +44-223-341-510
Email: Bob_Anderson.EuroPARC@rx.xerox.com

Andriessen, J.H. Erik, Department of Work and Organizational Psychology, Delft
University of Technology, Kanaalweg 2B, P.O.Box 5050, NL-
2600 GB Delft, The Netherlands.
Tel: +31-15-783-720   Fax: +31-15-782-950
Email: wmbpand@hdetud1.nl

Applegate, Lynda M., Harvard Business School, Loeb25, Soldiers Field Road, Boston,
MA 02163, USA.
Tel: +1-617-495-6362   Fax: +1-617-495-5277
Email: lapplegate@hbs.harvard.edu

Bannon, Liam, J., Centre for Innovation and Cooperative Technology, University of
Amsterdam, Grote Bickersstraat 72, 1013 KS Amsterdam,
The Netherlands.
Tel: +31-20-525-1250   Fax: +31-20-525-1211
Email: bannon@ooc.uva.nl

Belew, Richard, Department of Computer Science, University of California - San Diego,
La Jolla, CA 92093, USA.

Boland, Richard, J., Science and Technology, Case Western Reserve, 2040 Adelbert
Road, Cleveland, OH 44106, USA.

Bowers, John, Department of Psychology, University of Manchester, Oxford Road,
Manchester M13 9PL, UK.
Tel: +44-61-275-2000   Fax: +44-61-275-2588
Email: bowers@man.psy.ac.uk

Bringsrud, Kjell Age, USIT, University of Oslo, PO Box 1059, Blindern N-0316,
Oslo 3, Norway.
Tel: +47-2-453-486   Fax: +47-2-455-770
Email: k.a.bringsrud@use.uio.no

Brothers, Lawrence, Bellcore, Room RRC-1H225, 444 Hoes lane, Piscataway,
NJ 08854, USA.
Tel: +1-201-829-2000   Fax: +1-201-292-0067
Email: quasar@bellcore.com

CCTA, See Advanced Concepts Branch

Ciardiello, G., Ing. C. Olivetti & C. SPA, Via Jervis 77, I-10015 IVREA, Italy.
Tel: +39-125-528-918   Fax: +39-125-528-984

Cicu, A., Bull Italy, Via Laboratori Olivetti, I-20010 Pregnana Milanese (MI), Italy.
Tel: +39-2-933-682-64   Fax: +39-2-933-684-56

Clark, W.J., BT Laboratories, RT4321, Martlesham Heath, Ipswich, IP5 7RE, UK.
Tel: +44-473-642-006   Fax: +44-473-643-791
Email: clark_w_j@bt-web.british-telecom.co.uk

Clarke, David, Department of Psychology, University of Nottingham, University Park,
Nottingham, NG7 2RD, UK.
Tel: +44-602-484-848x3180 Fax: +44-602-590-339
Email: ddc@uk.ac.nott.psyc

Condon, Chris, BICC Systems Development Centre, Maylands Avenue,
Hemel Hempstead, HP2 4SJ, UK.
Tel: +44-442-210-100   Fax: +44-442-210-101
Email: fzbicdb@uk.ac.ucl

Co-Tech, See Speth (Rolf)

CSC Europe, Computer Sciences House, Brunel Way, Slough, SL1 1XL, UK.
Tel: +44-753-573-232   Fax: +44-753-576-788

CSCW Special Interest Group, UK, See Scrivener (Steve)

De Michelis, Giorgio, Dip. Scienze dell'Informazione, Universita di Milano,
Via Moretto 9, 20133 Milano, Italy.
Tel: +39-2-7575-221/209   Fax: +39-2-7611-0556
Email: demichelis@imiucca.bitnet

Dewan, Presun, Department of Computer Science, Purdue University, Hovde Hall,
West Lafayette, IN 47907, USA.
Tel: +1-317-494-6014   Fax: +1-317-494-0739
Email: pd@cs.purdue.edu

Durfee, Edmund, Electrical Engineer & Computer Science,Univ of Michigan Ann Arbor,
1101 Beal Avenue, Ann Arbor, MI 48109, USA.
Tel: +1-313-936-1563   Fax: +1-313-763-1260
Email: durfee@caen.engin.umich.edu

Eherer, Stefan, Lehrstuhl für Informatik V, RWTH Aachen, Ahornstr. 55, D-5100
Aachen, Germany.
Tel: +49-241-802-1516   Fax: +49-241-802-1529
Email: eherer@picasso.informatik.rwth-aachen.de

Ellis, Clarence (Skip), Department of Computer Science, University of Colorado, Boulder, Colorado 80309, USA.
Email: skip@colorado.edu

Endrizzi, Adriano, CEC - Joint Research Centre, I-21020 Ispra (VA), Italy.
Tel: +39-332-789-213   Fax: +39-332-789-098
Email: aendrizzi@cen.jrc.it

ESPRIT, See Metakides, G. (basic research) & Stajano, A. (pre-competitive research).

Finkelstein, Anthony, Department of Computing, Imperial College, 180 Queens Gate, London SW7 2BZ, UK.
Tel.+44-71-589-5111   Fax +44-71-581-8024
Email: acwf@uk.ac.ic.doc

Fischer, Gerhard, Gerhard Fischer, Department of Computer Science, University of Colorado, Boulder, Campus Box 430, Boulder, CO 80309, USA.
Tel: +1-303-492-1502   Fax: +1-303-492-2844
Email: gerhard@cs.colorado.edu

Fischer, Michael J., Computer Science, Yale University, Box 2158 Yale Station, New Haven, CT 06520-2158, USA.
Tel: +1-203-432-1270   Fax: +1-203-432-0593
Email: fischer-michael@cs.yale.edu

Foundation for Cooperative Work Technology, See Prinz (Wolfgang)

Gale, Stephen, Hewlett Packard Laboratories, Filton Road, Stoke Gifford, Bristol, Avon BS12 6QZ, UK.
Tel: +44-272-799-910   Fax: +44-272-790-554
Email: srg@hplb.hpl.hp.com

Gallupe, Brent, Queen's University, School of Business, Kingston, Ontario K7l 3N6, C
Tel: +1-613-545-2361   Fax: +1-613-545-2013
Email: gallupeb@qucdn.queensu.ca

Gibbs, Simon, Centre Universitaire d'Informatique, 12 rue du Lac, CH-1207, Geneva, Switzerland.
Tel: +41-22-787-65-87   Fax: +41-22-735-39-05
Email: simon@cui.unige.ch

Gilbert, Nigel, Social & Computer Sciences Research Group, Dept of Sociology, University of Surrey, Guildford GU2 5XH, UK.
Tel: +44 483-509-292   Fax: +44 483-300-803
Email: gng@soc.surrey.ac.uk

Grantham, Charles, Department of Organizational Studies, University of San Francisco Ignatian Heights, 2130 Fulton Street, San Francisco, CA 94117-1080 USA.
Tel: +1-415-666-2147   Fax: +1-415-666-2793
Email: well!cegrant@apple.com

Greenberg, Saul, Department of Computer Science, University of Calgary, Calgary, Alberta, T2N 1N4, Canada.
Tel: +1-403-220-6087   Fax: +1-403-284-4707
Email: saul@cpsc.ucalgary.ca

Greif, Irene, Lotus Development, 55 Cambridge Parkway, Cambridge MA 02142, USA.
Tel: +1-617-577-8500   Fax: +1-617-693-5552
Email: greif@lotus.uucp

Guest, Steve, Department of Computer Studies, Loughborough University of
Technology, Loughborough, Leicestershire, LE11 3TU, UK.
Tel: +44-509-222-692   Fax: +44-509-610-815
Email: s.p.guest@uk.ac.lut

Haberkorn, Brigitte, Technische Universität Wien, Institut für Angewandte Informatik,
Abteilung Datenbanken und Expertensysteme, Paniglgasse 16,
1040 Vienna, Austria.
Tel: +43-1-588-016-122   Fax: +43-1-505-53-54
Email: haber@vexpert.dbai.tuwien.ac.at

Haugeneder, Hans, Siemens AG, ZFE IS INF, Otto-Hahn-Ring 6, 8000 Munich 83,
Germany.
Tel: +49-89-636-43698   Fax: +49-89-636-42284
Email: hans%bloom%ztivax%unido@ztivax

Hicom, C/o LUTCHI, Department of Computer Studies, Loughborough University of
Technology, Loughborough, Leicestershire, LE11 3TU, UK.
Tel: +44-533-222-789   Fax: +44-533-610-815
Email: membership@uk.ac.lut.hicom

Hiltz, Starr Roxanne, Department of Computer & Information Science, Information
Technologies Centre, New Jersey Institute of Technology, Lock St
and Central Av., Newark, NJ 07102, USA.
Tel: +1-201-596-3388   Fax: +1-201-596-5777
Email: roxanne@eies2.njit.edu

Hirschheim, Rudy, Information Systems Research Center, College of Business
Administration, University of Houston, Houston, Texas 77204, USA.
Tel: +1-713-749-6762   Fax: +1-713-749 - 6765
Email: disct6@jetson.uh.edu

Holsapple, Clyde W., Department of Decision Science & Information Systems,
Business and Economics Building Room 317, University of
Kentucky, Lexington, KY 40506-0034, USA.
Tel: +1-606-257-5236   Fax: +1-606-257-8938
Email: holsappl@ukcc.bitnet

Hoschka, Peter, GMD-F3, POB 1240, D-5205 Sankt Augustin 1, Germany.
Tel: +49-22-41-14-27-16   Fax: +49-22-41-14-26-18
Email: hoschka@f3.gmd.dbp.de

Hough, Robbin, School of Business Administration, Oakland University, Rochester,
MI 48309-4401, USA.
Tel: +1-313-651-0820   Fax: +1-313-651-4071
Email: hough@unix.secs.oakland.edu

Hughes, Philip, BNR Europe Ltd., London Road, Harlow, Essex CM17 9NA, UK.
Tel: +44-279-429- 531   Fax: +44-279-441-551
Email: philip.j.hughes@bnr.co.uk

Humphreys, Patrick, Department of Social Psychology, London School of Economics,
Houghton St, London WC2A 2AE, UK.
Tel: +44-71-405-7686 x 3212/2714   Fax: +44-71-242-0392
Email: pch@lse-pims.uucp

Hutchison, David, DTI/ITD3, Room 806, Kingsgate House, 66-74 Victoria Street,
London SW1E 6SW, UK.
Tel: +44-71-215-8304   Fax: +44-71-828-1503
Email: dh@computing.lancaster.ac.uk

Ishii, Hiroshi, NTT Human Interface Laboratories, 1-2356 Take, Yokosuka-shi,
Kanagawa, 238-03, Japan.
Tel: +81-468-59-3522   Fax: +81-468-59-2332
Email: ishii%ntthif.ntt.jp@relay.cs.net

Jarke, Matthias, Lehrstuhl für Informatik V, RWTH Aachen, Ahornstr. 55,
5100 Aachen, Germany.
Tel: +49-241-802-1500   Fax: +49-241-802-1529
Email: jarke@picasso.informatik.rwth-aachen.de

Johansen, Robert, Institute for the Future, 2740 Sand Hill Road, Menlo Park,
California 94025-7097, USA.
Tel: +1-415-854-6322   Fax: +1-415-854-7850
Email: rjohansen (MCI mail) b.johansen (Applelink)

Johnson, Peter, Department of Computer Science, Queen Mary & Westfield College,
University of London, Mile End Road, London, E1 4NS, UK.
Tel: +44-71-975-5224   Fax: +44-81-980-6533
Email: pete@dcs.qmw.ac.uk

Kalliomaki, Sakari, Laboratory for Information Processing, Technical Research Centre
of Finland, Lehtisaarentie 2 A, SF-00340 Helsinki, Finland.
Tel: +358-0-4561   Fax: +358-0-489-519
Email: sakari.kalliomaki@vtt.fi

Kleinman, David, Department of Electrical Engineering, University of Connecticut,
Storrs, CT 06268, USA.

Kling, Rob, Information & Computer Science, University of California (Irvine), Irvine,
CA 92717, USA.
Tel: +1-714-856-5955   Fax: +1-714-856-4056
Email: kling@ics.uci.edu

Kluwer Academic Publishers, Spuiboulevard 50, PO Box 17, 3300 AA Dordrecht,
The Netherlands.
Tel: +31-78-334-911   Fax: +31-78-334-254
Email: surf404@kub.nl

Korte, Werner B., Empirica Gmbh, Kaiserstr. 37, D-5300 Bonn 1, Germany.
Tel: +49-228-267-9050   Fax: +49-228-210-279

Kraut, Robert, Room 2E-232, Bellcore, 445 South Street, Morristown, NJ 07962, USA.
Tel: +1-201-829-4513   Fax: +1-201-829-7019
Email: kraut@thumper.bellcore.com

Krcmar, Helmut, Institut für Betriebswirtschaftslehre (510 H), Universität Hohenheim,
Postfach 70 05 62, D-7000 Stuttgart 70, Germany.
Tel: +49-711-459-3345   Fax: +49-711-459-2785
Email: helmut.krcmar@rus.uni-stuttgart.de

Kreplin, Klaus, TA-Triumph-Adler AG, Abt. EF2, Fürther Str. 212,
D-8500 Nürnberg 80, Germany.
Tel: +49-911-322-6306   Fax: +49-911-322-6282
Email: kk@triumph-adler.de

Kuchinsky, Allan, Hewlett-Packard Laboratories, 1501 Page Mill Road, Palo Alto,
California 94304-1126, USA.
Tel: +1-415-857-7423   Fax: +1-415-857-8526
Email: kuchinsk@hplabs.hp.com

Kyng, Morten, Computer Science Department, Åarhus University, Bld. 540,
Ny Munkegade, DK-8000 Aarhus C, Denmark.
Tel.: +45-86-12-71-88   Fax: .+45-86-13-57-25
Email: mkyng@daimi.aau.dk

Lubich, Hannes, Institut fuer Technische Informatik und Kommunikationsnetze, Swiss
Federal Institute of Technology, Zuerich (ETHZ), ETH-Zentrum,
CH-8092 Zuerich, Switzerland.
Tel.: +41-1-254-7006   Fax: +41-1-262-3973
Email: lubich@komsys.tik.ethz.ch

Lyytinen, Kalle, University of Jyväskylä, Dept. of Computer Science and Information
Systems, PO Box 35, SF-40351, Jyväskylä, Finland.
Tel: +358-41-603-025   Fax: +358-41-603-611
Email: kalle@jytko.jyu.fi

Macaulay, Linda, Department of Computation, UMIST, PO Box 88, Manchester,
M60 1QD, UK.
Tel: +44-61-200-3354   Fax: +44-61-228-7386

Malone, Thomas W., Sloan School of Management, 50 Memorial Drive (E53-333),
Massachusetts Institute of Technology, Cambridge,
MA 02139, USA.
Tel: +1-617-253-6843   Fax: +1-617-258-7579
Email: malone@eagle.mit.edu

Mantei, Marilyn, Computer Systems Research Institute, University of Toronto,
10 Kings College Road, Toronto, Ontario M5S 1A4, Canada.
Tel: +1-416-978-5512   Fax: +1-416-978-4765
Email: mantei@dgp.toronto.edu

Marca, David, Digital Equipment Corporation, 110 Spit Brook Road, ZKO2-3/K06,
Nashua, NH 03062-2698, USA.
Tel: +1-603-881-1801   Fax: +1-603-881-1700
Email: marca@clt.enet.dec.com

Marschak, T., School of Business, University of California, Berkeley, CA 94720, USA.

Metakides, George, CEC/DG XIII, Rue de la Loi 200, Brussels 1049, Belgium.
Tel: +32-2-235-16-03   Fax: +32-2-235-38-21
Email: gmet@dg13.cec.be

Mich, Louisa, Instituto di Informatica, Universita degli Studi di Trento, Via Inama 13,
I-38100 Trento, Italy.
Tel: +39-461-882-123   Fax: +39-461-881-499
Email: mich@itn.cisti

Morris, James, Department of Computer Science, Carnegie-Mellon University,
Pittsburgh, PA 15213, USA.

Olerup, Agneta, Department of Information & Computer Science, Lund University,
Solvegatan 14a, S-223 62 LUND, Sweden.
Tel: +46-46-10-97-64   Fax: +46-46-10-47-28
Email: agneta.olerup@ibadb.lu.se

Olson, Gary, Cognitive Science & Machine Intelligence Lab, University of Michigan, 701
Tappan Street, Ann Arbor, MI 48109-1234, USA.
Tel: +1-313-747-4948   Fax: +1-313-936-3168
Email: gmo@csmil.umich.edu

O'Malley, Claire, Department of Psychology, University of Nottingham, University
Park, Nottingham NG7 2RD, UK.
Tel: +44-602-484-848x3892   Fax: +44 602-590-339
Email: com@uk.ac.psyc.nott

Pastor, Encarna, Department of Telematic Systems Engineering, ETSI Telecomunicacion,
Ciudad Universitaria, E-28040 Madrid, Spain.
Tel:+34-1-549-5700 ext.366 Fax: +34-1-543-2077
Email: encarna@dit.upm.es

Pehrson, Bjorn, SICS, Box 1263, S-164 28 Stockholm-Kista, Sweden.
Tel: +46 - 8-752-1510   Fax: +46 - 8-751-7230
Email: bjorn@sics.se

Perlin, Kenneth H., Computer Science, New York University, 251 Mercer Street,
New York, NY 10003, USA.

Pollitzer, Elizabeth, Department of Computing, Imperial College, 180 Queens Gate,
London SW7 2BZ, UK.
Tel: +44-71-589-5111 x 4981 Fax: +44-71-581-8024
Email: eep@doc.ic.ac.uk

Power, Richard, AIS S.p.A., Via Rombon 11, 20134 Milano, Italy.
Tel: +39-2-264-0107   Fax: +39-2-264-107-44

Prinz, Wolfgang, GMD, POB 1240, D-5205 Sankt Augustin 1, Germany.
Tel: +49-22-41-142-730   Fax: +49-22-41-142-084
Email: prinz@f3.gmd.dbp.de

RACE , See Torcato (Jose)

Radermacher, Franz J., FAW, Universitat Ulm, Helmholtzstrabe 16, Postfach 20 60,
D-7900 Ulm/Donau, Germany.
Tel: +49-731-501-100   Fax: +49-731-501999
Email: radermac@dulfawla.bitnet

Raman, K.S., Department of Information Systems and Computer Science, National
University of Singapore, Kent Ridge, 0510, Singapore.
Tel: +65-772-2911   Fax: +65-779-4580
Email: ramanks@nusvm.earn

Rao, Srinivasan (Chino), M.I.S. Division, Faculty of Commerce, 2053 Main Mall,
Vancouver, B.C., V6T 1Y8, Canada.
Tel: +1-604-224-8368   Fax: +1-604-224-8489
Email: usercrao@ubcmtsg.bitnet

Rein, Gail, Software Technology Programme, MCC, 3500 West Balcones Center Drive,
Austin, Texas 78759-6509, USA.
Tel: +1-512-338-3303   Fax: +1-512-338-3899
Email: rein@mcc.com

Robinson, Mike, Centre for Innovation & Co-operative Technology, University of
Amsterdam, Grote Bickersstraat 72, 1013 KS Amsterdam,
The Netherlands.
Tel: +31-20-525-1225/1250   Fax: +31-20-525-1211
Email: mike@ooc.uva.nl

Rodden, Tom, Department of Computing, University of Lancaster, Baillrig,
Lancaster LA1 4YR, UK.
Tel: +44-524-65201x3823   Fax: +44-524-381-707
Email: tam@uk.ac.lancs.comp

Rosenberg, Duska, Department of Computer Science, Brunel University, Uxbridge,
Middlesex UB8 3PH, UK.
Tel: +44-895-74000   Fax: +44-895-32806
Email: duska.rosenberg@brunel.ac.uk

Rosenberg, Laurence, Information, Robotics & Intelligent Systems Division, NSF,
1800 G St. NW, Washington, D.C. 20550, USA.
Tel: +1-202-357-9592   Fax: +1-202-357-0320
Email: lrosenbe@note2.nsf.gov

Ruedebusch, Tom D., Institute for Telematics, University of Karlsruhe, Zirkel 2,
W-7500 Karlsruhe, Germany.
Tel: +49-721-608-3414   Fax: +49-721-606-097
Email: tom@ira.uka.de

Schael, Thomas, RSO, Via Leopardi, 1, I - 20123 Milano, Italy.
Tel: +39-2-720-00583   Fax: +39-2-806-800
Email: schael@vdveer.cs.vu.nl

Schatz, Bruce, R., Community Systems Laboratory, Life Sciences South,
University of Arizona, Tucson, AZ 85721, USA.
Tel: +1-602-621-9174   Fax: +1-602-621-3709
Email: schatz@cs.arizona.edu

Schmidt, Kjeld, Cognitive Systems Laboratory, Risoe National Laboratory, PO Box 49,
DK-4000 Roskilde, Denmark.
Tel: +45-4237-1212   Fax: +45-4675-5170
Email: kschmidt@risoe.dk

Scrivener, Steve, LUTCHI, Department of Computer Studies, Loughborough University
of Technology, Leicestershire, LE11 3TU, UK.
Tel: +44-509-222-696   Fax: +44-509-610-815
Email: s.a.scrivener@uk.ac.lut

Sharples, Michael, School of Cognitive and Computing Sciences, University of Sussex,
Brighton, BN1 9QH, UK.
Tel: +44-273-678-393   Fax: +44-273-678-188
Email: mike@uk.ac.sussex.cogs

Shave, Michael, Department of Computer Science, University of Liverpool, PO Box 147,
Liverpool, L69 3BX, UK.
Tel: +44-51-794-3667   Fax: +44-51-794-3759
Email: mshave@uk.ac.liv.cs

Sherwood-Smith, Michael, Computer Science Department, University College Dublin,
IRL-Belfield, Dublin 4, Ireland.
Tel: +353-1-2693-244   Fax: +353-1-2697-262
Email: michael@csvax.ucd.ie

Smith, Hugh, Department of Computer Science, University of Nottingham,
University Park, Nottingham, NG7 2RD, UK.
Tel: +44-602-484-848x3647 Fax: +44-602-588-138
Email: h.smith@uk.ac.nott.cs

Smith, John B., Department of Computer Science, University of North Carolina,
Chapel Hill, NC 27599-3175, USA.
Tel: +1-919-962-1792   Fax: +1-919-962-1799
Email: jbs@cs.unc.edu

Speth, Rolf, CEC/DG XIII, BRE 11/236, Avenue d'Auderghem 45, 1040 Bruxelles,
Belgium.
Tel: +32-2 -236-0416   Fax: +32-2-235-0655
Email: rspeth@com.qz.se

Stajano, Attilio, CEC/DG XIII, Rue de la Loi 200, Brussels 1049, Belgium.
Tel: +32-2-235-16-03   Fax: +32-2-235-38-21
Email: asta@dg13.cec.be

Stamper, Ronald, School of Management Studies, University of Twente, PO Box 217,
7500 AE Enschede, The Netherlands.
Tel: +31-53-894-038   Fax: +31-53-357-956
Email: stamper@utwente.nl

Star, Susan Leigh, Department of Sociology and Social Anthropology,
University of Keele, Keele, Staffordshire ST5 5BG, UK.
Tel: 44-782-621-111 x 4041 Fax: +44-782-613-847
Email: soa03@keele.ac.uk

Stary, Christian, School of Computer Science, The State University of Florida at Miami,
University Park, Miami, Florida 33199, USA.
Tel: +1-305-348-2440   Fax: +1-305-348-3647
Email: stary@fiu.scs.edu

Stodolsky, David, Department of Computer Science, Bldg. 20.2, Roskilde University Center, Post Box 260, DK-4000 Roskilde, Denmark.
Tel: 45-46-75-77-11 x2138   Fax: +45-46-75-74-01
Email: david@ruc.dk

Stotts, David, Computer and Information Sciences Department, 310 CSE Building, University of Florida, Gainesville, FL 32611, USA.
Tel: +1-904-392-1526   Fax: +1-904-392-1220
Email: pds@cis.ufl.edu

Suchman, Lucy, Xerox Corporation, Palo Alto Research Center, 3333 Coyote Hill Road, Palo Alto, California 94304, USA.
Tel: +1-415 - 494 -4000   Fax: +1-415-494-4970
Email: suchman@parc.xerox.com

Torcato, Jose, TR61 0/10, Rue de la Loi 200, B-1040 Bruxelles, Belgium.
Tel: +32-2-236-35-37   Fax: +32-2-235-69-37
Email: jt@dg13.cec.be

Usenet, UKnet Support Group, Computing Laboratory, The University, Canterbury, Kent, CT2 7NF, UK.
Tel: +44-227-764-000 x 7568 Fax: +44-227-762-811
Email: uknet@ukc.ac.uk

Van der Veer, Gerrit, C., Free University, Department of Computer Science, De Boelelaan 1081 A, 1081 HV Amsterdam, The Netherlands.
Tel: +31-20-548-4405   Fax: +31-20-642-6275
Email: gerrit@cs.vu.nl

Waern, Yvonne, Department of Psychology, Stockholm University, S-106 91 Stockholm, Sweden.
Tel: +46-816-38-94   Fax: +46-815-93-42
Email: yw@psychmax.psychology.su.se

Watson, Rick, Department of Management, University of Georgia, Athens, GA 30602, USA.
Tel: +1-404-542-3706   Fax +1-404- 542-3743
Email: rwatson@ugabus.bitnet

Whinston, Andrew, Department of Management Science & Information Systems, CBA 5.202, University of Texas at Austin, Austin, TX 78712-1175, USA.
Tel: +1-512-471-8879   Fax: +1-512-471-3034
Email: abw@emx.utexas.edu

Wilbur, Sylvia, Department of Computer Science, Queen Mary & Westfield College, Mile End Road, London E1 4NS, UK.
Tel: +44-81-975-5202   Fax: +44-81-980-6533
Email: sylvia@cs.qmc.ac.uk

Wilson, Paul, CSC Europe, Computer Sciences House, Brunel Way, Slough, SL1 1XL, UK.
Tel: +44-753-573-232   Fax: +44-753-516-178
Email: wilson@cs.nott.ac.uk or paul_wilson@uk.ac.lut.hicom

Yu, Keh-Chiang, Associate Professor, Institute of Information Management, 1001 Ta Hsueh Road, Hsinchu 30050, Taiwan, R.O.C.
Tel: +886-35-712-121-4433 Fax: +886-35-715-544
Email: kcyu@twnctu01.bitnet

Appendix E   Recommended Reading

An annotated bibliography of computer supported cooperative work, Greenberg, S., SIGCHI Bulletin, July 1991; or in **Computer supported cooperative work and groupware** - see below; or as a continuously updated research report from the Department of Computer Science, University of Calgary, Calgary, Alberta, Canada.

Computer augmented teamwork, Bostrom, R., Watson, R., Kiney, S. (Eds.), Van Nostrand Reinhold, New York, 1992/93 (in preparation).

Computer based group communication - the AMIGO activity model, Pankoke-Babatz U. (ed), Ellis Horwood Limited, Chichester, UK, 1989.

Computer-supported cooperative work: A book of readings, Greif, I. (ed), Morgan Kaufmann Publishers, Hove, West Sussex, UK, 1988.

Computer supported cooperative work and groupware, Greenberg, S. (ed), Academic Press, London, 1991.

Computer support for cooperative work (working title), Bannon, L., Robinson, M. & Schmidt, K.(in preparation).

COSCIS'91 - Proceedings of the IFIP TC8 Working Conference on Collaborative Work, Social Communications and Information Systems, Stamper, R., Kerola, P., Lee, R. & Lyytinen, K. (Eds.), North-Holland Elsevier Science Publishers, 1991.

CSCW'86 - Proceedings of the Conference on Computer-Supported Cooperative Work, Peterson, D. (ed), Austin, Texas, December 1986. MCC Software Technology Program, Austin, Texas,USA, 1986 (out of print).

CSCW'88 - Proceedings of the Conference on Computer-Supported Cooperative Work, Portland, Oregan, September 1988 (ACM Order Department, PO Box 64145, Baltimore, MD 21264. Order No 612880).

CSCW'90 - Proceedings of the Conference on Computer-Supported Cooperative Work, Los Angeles, California, October 1990 (ACM Order Department, PO Box 64145, Baltimore, MD 21264. Order No 612900).

Design at work: cooperative design of computer systems, Greenbaum, J. & Kyng, M. (Eds), Lawrence Erlbaum Associates, 1991.

EC-CSCW'89 - Proceedings of the 1st European Conference on Computer Supported Cooperative Work, Gatwick, London, UK, 1989 (out of print) (many of these papers were published in **Studies in computer supported cooperative work** - see below)

ECSCW'91 - Proceedings of the 2nd European Conference on Computer-Supported Cooperative Work, Bannon, L.J., Robinson, M. & Schmidt, K. (Eds), September 25-27, 1991, Amsterdam, The Netherlands (available from Sageforce Ltd, (ECSCW'91), 61 Kings Road, Kingston-upon-Thames, Surrey, KT2 5JA, UK.

Groupware, Johansen, R., The Free Press, Collier Macmillan Publishers, London,1988

Intellectual teamwork: social and technological foundations of cooperative work, Galegher, J., Kraut, R. & Egido, C., Erlbaum, NJ, 1990.

In the age of the smart machine, Zuboff, S., Basic Books Inc, New York, 1988.

Leading business teams, Johansen, R. et al, Addison-Wesley, Reading, Massachusetts, 1991.

Multi-user interfaces and applications - Proceedings of the IFIP WG8.4 Conference on Multi-user Interfaces and Applications, Heraklion, Crete, Greece, 24-29 September, 1990; Gibbs, S. & Verrijn-Stuart, A.A. (Eds), North-Holland, Amsterdam, 1990.

Proceedings of the international workshop on CSCW, 9-11 April, Berlin, Gorling, K. and Sattler, C. (eds), Institut fuer Informatik und Rechentechnik, Informatik, Informationen, Reporte 6 (1991) 4, Rudower Chaussee 5, Berlin, 1199, Germany.

Plans and situated actions, Suchman, L. A., Cambridge University Press, 1987.

Selected papers from the conference on computer-supported cooperative work (CSCW'88), ACM Transactions on Office Information Systems, Volume 6, No 4, October 1988, ACM, New York.

Shared minds, Schrage, M., Random House, 1990.

Socializing the human-computer environment, Vaske, Jerry, J. & Grantham, Charles, E., Ablex, Norwood, NJ, 1990.

Special issue on the language/action perspective, ACM Transactions on Office Information Systems, Volume 6, No 2, April 1988, ACM, New York.

Special issues on computer supported cooperative work and groupware, the International Journal of Man-Machine Studies, Volume 34, Nos 2 (February 1991) and 3 (March 1991), Academic Press.

Studies in computer supported cooperative work - theory, practice and design, Bowers J.M. & Benford S.D. (eds), North Holland Elsevier Publishers, Amsterdam, 1991. (NB. This includes most of the proceedings of the 1st European CSCW conference, EC-CSCW'89).

Technology and the transformation of white-collar work, Kraut R. E. (ed), Lawrence Erlbaum Associates, New Jersey and London,1987.

Technology for teams: enhancing productivity in networked organizations, Opper S. and Fersko-Weiss H., Van Nostrand Reinhold, New York, 1991.

The network nation, Hiltz S R and Turoff M, Addison-Wesley, Massachusetts, 1978.

Understanding computers and cognition, Winograd T and Flores F, Ablex Publishing Corporation, 1986.

CSCW: theory, technology and applications (working title), Rodden, T. & Benford, S. (Eds), IEE Computing Series, Peter Peregrinus, Stevenage, UK, (in preparation).

Appendix F References

1   **CSCW: Four characters in search of a context**, Bannon L. & Schmidt K., Ed. Bowers, J.M. & Benford, S.D. (eds), in Studies in Computer Supported Cooperative Work (selected papers from the 1st European CSCW conference, Gatwick, London, UK, 13-15 Sep 1989). North Holland Elsevier Science Publishers, 1991.

2   **Groupware**, Johansen R., Free Press, New York, 1988.

3   **The way we work**, Network magazine, pp. 24-27, April 1988.

4   **Conference Chair's message**, Krasner, H., in: Peterson, D., (ed), CSCW'86 - Proceedings of the Conference on Computer-Supported Cooperative Work (MCC Software Technology Program, Austin, Texas, 1986).

5   **Beyond the Data Processing Horizon**, Hammar, Carl, Education and Computing 1, 1985, pp. 147-154, North Holland.

6   **Group decision support systems: a new frontier**, DeSanctis, G.L. and Gallupe, R.B., Database (16:2), pp. 3-9, Winter 1985.

7   **Computer-based systems for cooperative work and group decisionmaking: Status of use and problems in development**, Kraemer K L and King J L, in CSCW'86 Proceedings - see (4) for full reference.

8   **Design and use of high-speed networks in multi-media applications**, Hopper, A., 3rd IFIP Conference on High Speed Networking, Berlin, March 1991.

9   **Relevance of the X.500 directory to CSCW applications: directory support for computer based group communication**, Prinz W, & Pennelli P, in Studies in Computer Supported Cooperative Work - see (1) for full reference.

10 **The videoWindow system in informal communication**, Fish, R.S., Kraut, R.E. and Chalfonte, B.L., In Proceedings of the Conference on Computer-Supported Cooperative Work, Los Angeles, California, October 1990 (ACM Order Department, PO Box 64145, Baltimore, MD 21264. Order No 612900).

11 **Rendezvous: An architecture for syncronous multi-user applications**, Patterson J.F., Hill, R.D., Rohall, S.L. and Meeks, W.S., in CSCW'90 Proceedings - see (10) for full reference.

12 **Experiences in designing the Hohenheim CATeam Room**, Ferwagner, T., Wang, Y., Lewe, H. & Krcmar,H., in Studies in Computer Supported Cooperative Work - see (1) for full reference.

13 **WYSIWIS Revised: Early experiences with multi-user interfaces**, Stefik, M., Bobrow, D.G., Lanning, S., & Tatar, D., in CSCW'86 Proceedings - see (4) for full reference.

14 **A performing medium for working group graphics,** Lakin, F., in CSCW'86
Proceedings - see (4) for full reference.

15 **Intermedia: Issues, Strategies and Tactics in the design of a hypermedia
document system,** Garrett, N.L., Smith, K.E. and Meyrowitz,
N., in the Proceedings of CSCW'88, September 26-29, 1988,
Portland, Oregon. Association of Computing Machinery, P.O.Box
64145, Baltimore, MD 21264, USA. ACM order No 612880.

16 **Supporting Collaboration in NOTECARDS** Trigg R, Suchman L, Halasz F, in
CSCW'86 Proceedings - see (4) for full reference.

17 **Why groupware is gaining ground,** Esther Dyson, Datamation, 1 March 1990.

18 **Pulling together,** Durham, T., IBM System User, October 1990.

19 **Local and global structuring of computer mediated communication:
developing linguistic perspectives on CSCW in
Cosmos,** Bowers, J. & Churcher, J., in CSCW'88 proceedings -
see (15) for full reference.

20 **ORDIT: a cooperative methodology for the definition of organisational
requirements,** Olphert C.W. & Powrie S.E., in proceedings of
the IFIP 8.4 conference on multi-user interfaces and applications,
Haraklion, Crete, 24-26 September, 1990.

21 **Preliminary procedure for Group Work Design in central government
departments, version 1.1,** Bowers J., Advanced Concepts
Branch, CCTA, Riverwalk House, Millbank, SW1P 4RT, UK.
January 1991.

22 **ICICLE: Groupware for code inspection,** Brother, L., Sembugamoorthy, V.
and Muller, M., in CSCW'90 proceedings - see (10) for full
reference.

23 **CoAuthor - a hypermedia group authoring environment,** Hahn, U., Jarke,
M., Eherer, S. and Kreplin, K., in Studies in Computer
Supported Cooperative Work - see (1) for full reference.

24 **A Group Decision Support System for Idea Generation and Issue
Analysis in Organisational Planning** Applegate L M,
Konsynski B R and Nunamaker J F, in CSCW'86 proceedings -
see (4) for full reference.

25 **Report on a development project use of an issue-based information
system,** Burgess Yakemovic, K.C. and Conklin, E.J., in
CSCW'90 proceedings -see (10) for full reference.

26 **Tools Help People Co-operate only to the Extent that they Help them
Share Goals and Terminology,** Neches R, in CSCW'86
proceedings - see (4) for full reference.

27 **Understanding computers and cognition,** Winograd T and Flores F, Ablex
Publishing Corporation, 1986).

28 **The temporal structure of cooperative activity,** Reder S. and Schwab, R.G., in CSCW'90 proceedings - see (10) for full reference.

29 **Plans and situated actions,** Suchman, L. A., Cambridge University Press, 1987.

30 **More than just a communication system: Diversity in the use of electronic mail,** Mackay, W. E., in CSCW'88 proceedings - see (15) for full reference.

31 **Groupware, some issues and experiences,** Ellis, C.A., Gibbs, S.J. and Rein, G.L., Communications of the ACM, Vol 34, No 1, January 1991.

32 **Addressing in an Office Procedure System,** Kreifelts T and Seuffert P, in the proceedings of the IFIP 6.5 International Working Conference on Message Handling Systems, Munich, April 1987, North Holland.

33 **Creative organization theory,** Morgan, G, Sage Publications, 1989.

34 **Cognitive Science and Organizational Design: A Case Study of Computer Conferencing,** Crowston K, Malone T W and Lin F, in CSCW'86 proceedings - see (4) for full reference.

35 **Diplans: A new Language for the study and implementation of Coordination,** Holt, Anatol W., ACM Transactions on Office Information Systems, Vol6 No2, April 1988.

36 **Requirements of activity management,** Benford S., in Studies in Computer Supported Cooperative Work - see (1) for full reference.

37 **Can networks make an organisation?,** Berman T, & Thorensen K, in CSCW'88 proceedings - see (15) for full reference.

38 **Designing for a dollar a day,** Kyng, M., in CSCW'88 proceedings - see (15) for full reference.

39 **Cooperative prototyping studies - users and designers,** Bødker S. & Grønbæk K., in Studies in Computer Supported Cooperative Work - see (1) for full reference.

40 **A methodological approach to Computer Supported Cooperative Work,** Schäl T. & Zeller B., in the proceedings of the fifth European conference on Cognitive Ergonomics, ECCE-5, Urbino, Italy, 3-6 September, 1990.

41 **A framework for studying research collaboration** Suchman L and Trigg R, in CSCW'86 proceedings - see (4) for full reference.

42 **The Network Nation,** Hiltz S R and Turoff M, Addison-Wesley, Massachusetts, 1978

43 **The dynamics of small group decision making using e-mail,** Fafchamps D, Reynolds D, Kuchinsky A, in Studies in Computer Supported Cooperative Work - see (1) for full reference.

44   **Harmonious working and CSCW: Computer technology and air traffic control**, Harper R A, in Studies in Computer Supported Cooperative Work - see (1) for full reference.

45   **Wired for action**, Jack Schofield, The Guardian, UK, Thursday 30 November 1989.

46   **PC..Phone Home**, Martin Banks, Portable Computer Review, June 1990.

47   **Report Cards**, MacUser USA, July 1990, p. 103.

48   **The use of Computer Networks for Education and Training**, Robin Mason (Open University), The Training Agency, Moorfoot, Sheffield S1 4PQ, UK. 1989.

49   **Inter-personal organisers**, PC Magazine, December 1989.

50   **A Groupware Toolbox**, Opper, Susanna, Byte Magazine, Dec 1989, pp. 275-282.

51   **Timbuktu 3.1**, MacUser UK, September 1990.

52   **Workgroup Software**, Simon Collin, Which Computer, UK, June 1990.

53   **Mac means big business**, MacUser, UK, 7th September 1990.

54   **Projecting the right image**, Business Systems & Equipment Magazine, Feb 1990.

55   **The decision-making progress**, Stephen Ward, The Guardian, UK, 21 Sep 1990.

56   **Towards a national collaboratory**, Lederberg, J. & Uncapher, K., Report of a workshop at Rockefeller University, March 17-18, 1989. National Science Foundation, 1800 G St. NW, Washington, D.C. 20550, USA. 1990.

57   **What is Coordination Theory and how can it help design cooperative work systems?**, Malone, Thomas W. & Crowston, K., in CSCW'90 proceedings - see (10) for full reference.

58   **Organisation theory - selected readings**, Pugh, D.S., Penguin Books Limited, 2nd edition, 1984.

59   **Introduction to psychology**, Hilgard, E.R., Atkinson, R.L. & Atkinson, R.C., Harcourt Brace Jovanovich Inc, New York, 7th edition, 1979.

Index

ACB - see Advanced Concepts Branch
ACM 11, 12, 97, 104
Activity processing 27, 28, 29, 37, 41, 42,
     44, 45, 46, 97
Administrative support personnel 41, 46
Advanced Concepts Branch 1, 3, 4, 9, 34, 36,
     48, 49, 50, 97, 104
Agents 17, 59, 60, 61, 62, 64, 66, 67, 70, 87,
     88 (see also Intelligent agents)
Anthropology 4, 7, 30, 32, 57, 97
Archaeology 61
Argumentation tools 28, 29, 37, 80, 98
Artificial intelligence 56, 59, 60, 61, 67, 75
Brainstorming 26, 37, 54, 90, 98
Bulletin boards 13, 51, 92 (see also Computer
     conferencing)
Business needs 9, 36, 44, 48
Business trends 9, 33, 40
Calendar systems 9, 10, 11, 51, 98
CCTA 1, 4, 9, 34, 36, 48, 49, 50, 75, 104, 105
CD-ROM 27, 97
Clerical work 41, 46, 74
Co-authoring 10, 28, 29, 48, 52, 62, 65, 75,
     79, 84, 85, 90, 92, 93, 98
CO-TECH 14, 56
Cognitive ergonomics 57
Cognitive psychology 30, 98
Cognitive science 17, 61, 62, 63, 66, 75, 93
Collaboration research 7, 32, 36, 69, 70, 72,
     73, 75, 93, 94, 98
Collaboration technology 2, 18, 38, 66, 68, 93
Collaborative design 17, 56, 64, 66, 67, 72,
     73, 86, 90
Collaboratory 12, 69, 98
Commercial/industrial organisations
     Acorn Computers 58
     Action Technologies Inc 50
     Advertel Communication Systems 51
     AEG Olympia 58
     AIS 59, 60
     Alcatel CIT 59
     Alphatech 64
     Amper 59
     Arthur Andersen 66
     Bellcore 23, 87
     BICC Technologies 19, 70
     Bikit-Babbage Institute 60
     BNR Europe 19, 59, 71
     Brameur 61, 73
     Broderbund Software Inc 52
     BT 50, 59, 72
     Bull 58, 59, 85
     CE Software 50
     Chorus Systems 58

CLS Computer Lernsysteme 59
CMSU 59
CNET 59
CNRS 59
Compulink 51
Creon Application Development 58
CSC Europe 5, 9, 19, 50, 71, 105
Cselt-Centro 59
Custom 53
Dansk Internationalt 58
Datamont 85
Davis 54
Decision Dynamics Ltd 54
*Digital Equipment Corporation (DEC) 6,
     23, 50, 66, 84, 88*
Electricity Council Research Centre 61
Elsevier Science Publishers 59
Emmepi 60
Empirica 59
Enable Inc 53
Enea 58
Espasa Calpe 59
EuroPARC 20, 73
Farallon 52
FCMC 51
Fraunhofer Institute 59
GMD 21, 59, 76
Great Belt 59
Greyhawk 54
Group Technologies Inc 54
GRS 58
Harlequin 58
Hewlett-Packard Laboratories 19, 23, 72, 88
Human Technology 61, 73
ICL 51, 53, 54, 61, 73
IGC-Inspection Y Garantia de Calidad 58
Industrias de Telecomunication 60
Information Research Corporation 55
Institute for the Future 24, 89
Intrasoft 60
Iriam 59
Ispra 21, 59, 77
Jydsk Telefon 58, 59
Lombardia Informatica 60
Lotus Development Inc 52
Mari Computer Systems 60
MCC 24, 66, 90
Metasystems Design Group Inc 51
Motorola Computer Systems 53
Netmap Limited 55
Nixdorf 85
NTT 25, 96
Oeva-Versicherungen 59
Office Workstations Limited 52

Olivetti 58
PARC 25, 94
Philips 58
Plessey Research 60
Powercore Inc 51
PTT Research Neher Labs 59
Rank Xerox 20, 73
Realace 59
Risoe National Laboratory 21, 58, 77
RSO 21, 78
Rutherford Appleton Laboratory 59
Scaitech 58
SGS-Thomson 58
ShareData Inc 53
Siemens 60
Standard Elektrik Lorenz 59
Steria 60
Studsvik Nuclear 58
Swedish Institute of Computer Science 21, 78
SwixTech 55
TA-Triumph-Adler 21, 58, 59, 78
TDS Ltd. 60, 72
Technical Research Centre of Finland 21, 58, 79
Tecnatom 58
Tecnicas Reunidas 58
Tecograf Software 59
Telefonica Investigacion Y Desarrollo 59
Uitesa 58
Unisys 51
Ventana 54
X-Tel Services 59
Xerox 20, 25, 73, 94
Commitment making 7, 29, 35, 40, 98
Communication overload 47
Communication systems 26, 28, 33, 37, 43, 44, 73
Compression systems 9, 28, 33, 98
Computer conferencing 10, 13, 26, 30, 32, 41, 46, 48, 50, 51, 52, 83, 92, 99
Computer science 61, 62, 63, 64, 65, 66, 70, 71, 72, 75, 80, 81, 82, 83, 84, 85, 86, 88, 91, 94
Consensus 81, 85, 86
Coordination science 89
Coordination technology 4, 13, 18, 28, 35, 41, 99
Coordination theory 7, 18, 64, 68, 90, 95, 99
COST 14 Action 14
CSC Europe 5, 9, 19, 50, 71, 105
CSCW
benefits 43, 48
conferences 4, 5, 6, 7, 11
cost 2, 43
definition 6

environment 29, 56, 84
journals 12, 13
market trends 89
products 9, 34, 35, 36, 40, 50
reference model 57
risks 43
special interest group 12
Culture 31, 34, 37, 42, 84, 92, 95
Customer service 39, 42, 45
Decision making 16, 37, 44, 66, 68, 76, 77, 80, 83, 84, 86, 88, 91, 92, 95
Decision support systems 4, 7, 9, 11, 12, 28, 29, 37, 44, 66, 67, 68, 90, 92, 95
Desktop conferencing 99
Desktop video conferencing 2, 26, 34, 36, 37, 39, 40, 42, 59, 70, 71, 72, 73, 89, 94, 95, 96, 99
Discourse analysis 30, 99
Distance learning 16, 42, 45, 46, 99
DTI 17
EDI 87, 93
Electronic mail 2, 10, 11, 26, 30, 31, 33, 36, 42, 50, 52, 89, 92, 99
Email - see Electronic mail
Enabling technologies 6, 8, 26, 33
ESPRIT 15, 16, 58
ESRC 17, 97
Executives 39, 45
Foundation for Cooperative Work Technology 11
Game theory 86
GDSS - see Group decision support systems
Group activity support systems 26, 27, 29, 31, 34, 40, 43, 100
Group behaviour 32, 55, 95
Group decision support systems (GDSS) 11, 54, 73, 92, 100
Group dynamics aspects 32, 36, 100
Group knowledge development 56, 71
Group performance 32, 36, 88
Group processes 8, 90
Group work design 29, 31, 32, 36, 48, 56, 61, 71, 73, 74, 81, 82, 83, 87
Group work design procedure (GWDP) 36, 75, 100
Groupware 4, 6, 7, 85, 89, 93, 100
GWDP - see Group work design procedure
HICOM 13, 107
Human communication 30, 35, 96
Human-computer interaction 13, 17, 32, 76
Hypertext 27, 29, 52, 64, 70, 73, 79, 82, 86, 90, 95, 100
Idea generation 10, 28, 29, 30, 40, 79
Individual aspects 30, 35, 43
Information overload 47
Integrated packages 11, 53

Intelligent agents 59, 60, 61, 64, 66, 67 (see also Agents)
Intelligent whiteboards 27, 28
Interface design 30, 58, 68, 91, 96
ISDN 2, 4, 33, 34, 53, 59, 96, 100
Issue-based information systems 90
Knowledge development 71
Knowledge representation 62
Linguistics 4, 7, 30, 57, 101
Management issues 31
Management science 31, 64, 87, 92
Managers 39, 45
Manual workers 42, 46
Meeting room systems 11, 27, 35, 40, 41, 43, 45, 49, 54, 57, 81, 82, 87, 90, 91, 93, 101
Methodologies 27, 31, 32, 36, 57, 61, 62, 73, 74, 78, 82, 83, 87
MRC 17, 97
Multimedia 17, 27, 33, 56, 58, 59, 61, 70, 72, 73, 76, 77, 78, 84, 89, 96, 101
Naming tools 28, 29, 101
Networks 4, 13, 28, 29, 33, 34, 49, 69, 78, 82, 94, 100
NSF 18, 63
Operations research 64, 67
Organisation design 7, 13, 31, 101
Organisation theory 67, 101
Organisational aspects 31, 35, 43
Organisational behaviour 86, 95
Organisational change 31, 38, 44, 63, 71, 87
Organisational knowledge 17, 31, 63
Organisational learning 13, 86
Pilot studies 35, 48
Portable personal computers 35, 37, 38, 59, 78
Pragmatics 30, 101
Privacy 47
Procedure processing 2, 7, 27, 29, 34, 40, 41, 44, 45, 46, 51, 52, 101
Professionals 40, 45
Projects
    Academic institutional memory 63
    Adoption of team technology 92
    AIDAI 86
    Aide-de-Camp 61
    Amigo 75, 80, 82
    Amsterdam meeting environment 81
    ANSA 71
    Answer garden 89
    Assisting computer 76
    Automation of air traffic control 74
    CAFKA 85
    CAVECAT 94
    CHAOS 84
    Co-authoring and commenting support 65
    CoAUTHOR 79

Collaboration in software development 79
Collaborative software engineering 66
Collaborative writing 62, 75
COMDEC 88
COMMPOSITE 56
COMmunication in DECision Making 88
Comparison of team technologies 92
Computer aided team room (CATeam Room) 82
Computer audio video enhanced collaboration and telepresence 94
Computer support to promote cooperation 84
Consensus journals 85
Cooperation between mechanical designers and production planners 86
Cooperation of dispersed teams 61
Cooperative multimedia processes 56
Cooperative problem-solving at construction sites 78
Cooperative requirements capture 61, 73
Coordinating multi-processor organizations 64
Coordination in information systems 68
Coordination theory and technology 90
Cosmos 71, 73, 74, 75
COTERM 80
Cross-cultural analysis 92
CSCW environment 56
CSCW in small businesses 93
CSCW market trends 89
CSCW systems design concepts 56
Cultural influences on GDSS design 95
Database requirements for CSCW 74
DECO 56
DIMUN 70
DISSPRO 79
Distributed artificial intelligence 61
Distributed cooperative work 59
Distributed decision making 66
Distributed group decision making 68
Distributed international manufacturing 70
Distributed meetings 57
ELO 59
Elusive office 59
Emergence of social complexity 61
Emergency management 58
EUROCOOP 60, 71
Evaluating asyncronous communication 76
Executive 2000 92
Facilitation and leadership 92
GAUCHO 80
gIBIS 90
GRACE 75
Graphic coordination languages 95
Group collaboration in a collaboratory 69
Group interaction environment 83
Group work design procedure 75

GroupSketch 91
Groupware users' project 89
GroupWriter 92
GROVE 90
Growing organizational memories 89
ICICLE 87
IMAGINE 60
IMS 93
INFOKIT 85
INTACT 57
Intelligent agents 59
Intelligent folders 95
Interdisciplinary theory 57
Interface requirements 58
Interfaces for collaborative work 68
ISEM 58, 77
Issue-based information systems 90
ITHACA 85
ITSforGK 56, 87
Knowledge development 56
Knowledge-based systems as a
   communication mechanism 86
KWICK 59
MacAll 75
Media management toolkit 89
Meetings-that-WorkTM 88
MIAS 59
MILAN 70
Mobile PC 78
Models of cooperative work 60, 80
Models of human work activities 77
MOHAWC 77
Multi-agent environment 60
Multi-reader distributed hypertext 70
MultiG 78
Multimedia applications in high speed
   networks 78
Multimedia desktop conferencing 77
Multimedia industrial LAN 70
Multimedia office workstation 58
Multimedia teleconference system 96
Multimedia user modelling 61
MultiMETH 76
Multiparty desktop video conferencing 59
MULTIWORKS 58, 71, 79
MUMS 72
Negotiation protocol for intelligent agents
   67
NESTOR 84
Nick 90
Norm based management 87
Object lens 89
Organisational knowledge 63
Organizational computing development
   environment 94
Outlook 89

PECOS 60, 80
POGO 93
Practical constraints on decision making 67
PREP 65
Principles for CSCW product development 80
Professional community support 71
Reference model for CSCW 57
RepGrid-Net 92
Representing/supporting coordination 64
Requirements for remote cooperation 60, 72
ROCOCO 60, 72
SAMPO 83, 87
Samtek 86
Semi-structured messaging 88
Share 91
Social knowledge representation 62
SOFIA 84
Strudel 88
Subway coordinating system 95
Support for code inspection meetings 87
Support for collaborative workgroups 66
Support for group decision making 86
Support for network management 74
Support of authoring and learning 84
Supporting collaborative design 67
Survey of groupware use 93
Synchronous collaboration 93
System designer/end user communication 86
Systems technology for a collaboratory 69
Team creativity 92
Team development 92
TeamworkStation 96
The ordering of group opinions 93
The problem of joint action 61
Theory of coordination 64
TMPI 72
TOOLCRIB 93
U-CERAMICS 58
User requirements for multimedia 76
VideoWindow 87
Visual teleconsulting system 96
Prototyping 32, 48, 49, 70, 79, 80, 101
Psychology 4, 7, 61, 64, 66, 74, 75, 84, 85,
   94, 101
RACE 16
Repertory grid 92
Screen sharing 10, 27, 28, 31, 48, 52, 54, 69,
   81, 91, 96, 102
Secretarial and administrative workers 41, 46
SERC 17, 97
Shared databases 10, 11, 27, 29, 34, 37, 39,
   41, 44, 45, 46, 48, 52, 102
Shared information systems 26, 27, 29, 34,
   43, 52, 102
Shared screens - see Screen sharing
Shared work space systems 26, 28, 34, 43, 102

Social norms 87
Social psychology 32, 57, 63, 75, 102
Social science 80
Sociology 4, 7, 32, 57, 61, 94, 102
Software development process 35, 79, 87, 88, 93, 102
Software engineering 57, 66, 74
Speech act theory 30, 83, 84, 102
Team development/management tools 11, 55
Teamwork 2, 9, 36, 38, 42, 44, 83, 84, 92
Technicians 41, 46
Technology for teams 7
UK advanced technology programme 17, 60
UK joint council initiative 17, 61
Universities
  Åarhus 22, 59, 81
  Aachen 21, 79
  Amsterdam 22, 57, 81
  Arizona 69
  British Columbia 24, 91
  Brunel 19, 71
  Calgary 24, 91
  California - Berkeley 64
  California - Irvine 68
  California - San Diego 63
  Cambridge 61
  Carnegie Mellon 65
  Case Western Reserve 66
  Chiao Tung 25, 95
  Colorado 67
  Connecticut 64
  Delft 20, 75
  Duke 64
  Essex 61
  ETH 21, 76
  Florida - Gainesville 70
  Florida - Miami 23, 88
  Geneva 22, 82, 85
  Georgia 24, 92
  Glasgow 59
  Hohenheim 22, 57, 82
  Houston 24, 92
  Imperial College 60, 62
  Jyvaskyla 22, 83
  Kaiserslautern 84
  Karlsruhe 22, 83
  Keele 60
  Lancaster 20, 74
  Linkoeping 85
  Liverpool 61
  London School of Economics 63
  Loughborough 20, 60, 61, 72, 73
  Lund 22, 84
  Madrid 21, 60, 80
  Manchester 20, 74
  Maryland 70

Michigan 25, 66, 67, 93
Milan 23, 59, 84
MIT 6, 24, 64, 89
New Jersey Institute of Technology 68
New York 68
North Carolina - Chapel Hill 69
Nottingham 20, 61, 75
Oakland 25, 93
Purdue 66
Queen Mary & Westfield College 20, 61, 72
Queen's 24, 90
Rijks, Leiden 60
Roskilde 23, 85
Singapore 25, 92, 95
Stockholm 23, 85
Surrey 61
Sussex 20, 62, 75
Texas 25, 87, 93
Toronto 25, 94
Trento 23, 86
Twente 23, 87
UMIST 20, 61, 73
University College Dublin 22, 82
Uppsala 86
Vienna 22, 80
Yale 67
Usability testing 32, 48, 49, 103
Usenet 13
User involvement 31, 48, 80, 103
Video conferencing 8, 9, 32, 33, 49, 83, 103
  see also Desktop video conferencing
Video mail 26
Video windows 87
Voice mail 26
Wall screens 26, 28, 29, 35, 41, 42, 54, 103
Work flow systems 10, 27, 29, 34, 40, 41, 45, 46, 51
Work practices 30, 64, 74, 94
Workgroup computing 6, 7, 103
X.400 10, 28, 33, 103
X.500 26, 28, 31, 35, 103